JUDO
Techniques and Tactics
(Contest Judo)

JUDO
Techniques and Tactics
(Contest Judo)

ERIC
DOMINY

Illustrated by PETER JOHNSON

DOVER PUBLICATIONS, INC.

NEW YORK

This Dover edition, first published in 1969, is an unabridged and unaltered republication of the work originally published in 1966 under the title *Judo. Contest Techniques and Tactics*. The work is reprinted by special arrangement with Sterling Publishing Company, Inc., publisher of the original edition.

Standard Book Number: 486-22310-8
Library of Congress Catalog Card Number: 73-97503

Manufactured in the United States of America
Dover Publications, Inc.
180 Varick Street
New York, N.Y. 10014

To George W. Chew
my friend and Co-Founder of
the London Judo Society

Contents

Contents

ACKNOWLEDGMENTS

I wish to express my sincere thanks to Irving Farren—without whose help in editing this book it could not have been published—and to Jeff Smallcombe and William Taylor, who so patiently assisted me with the photographs from which the illustrations were prepared.

CHAPTER I

Contest Judo Generally

Procedure

Those for whom this book is intended will no doubt have gained some knowledge and even actual experience of the way in which a judo contest is conducted—be it only the contest which concludes a first grading examination. Important as it is to those taking part, however, that first grading contest is usually very informal. It is as the judoman progresses through the grades and on to inter-club matches, open tournaments and the trials from which national teams are selected that the contests become increasingly important and correspondingly more formal. And it is no exaggeration to say that the ceremonial preceding such contests is considered as important as the contests themselves. For this reason, I feel it is worth while outlining here what takes place at any major contest anywhere in the world.

To set the scene let us visualise a large hall, in the centre of which is the thirty-foot-square contest mat, surrounded by smaller mats to form a safety area—and seeming gigantic after club judo. Seated at a table to one side of the mat are the recorder, the timekeeper and other officials. Behind them sit the guests of honour.

The proceedings open with the referee and the two judges walking up to the mat on the side opposite the guests. They step on to the mat and bow to the occupants of the places of honour. The referee takes a step back and the judges bow to him before taking their seats at opposite corners of the mat.

Now the first contestants are called. For the purpose of easy identification by the judges, one will be wearing a white belt and the other a red belt in addition to the belts which show their grades. They step on to the mat from opposite sides and advance towards the centre until they are about twelve feet apart, at which point they stop, turn and, together, bow to the guests of honour. Then they bow to each other and await the referee's call of *"Hajime"* ("Commence"), which is made as soon as the referee is satisfied that the judges and timekeeper are also ready.

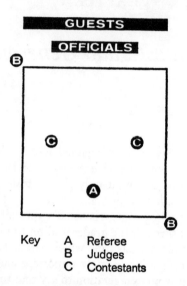

| GUESTS |
| OFFICIALS |

Key A Referee
      B Judges
      C Contestants

It must be assumed that, for their own benefit, the contestants have thoroughly acquainted themselves with the contest rules—which, though lengthy and seemingly complicated, are based on sound common sense.

One point (*ippon*) decides a contest, and this must be scored within the time prescribed by the organisers of the event, which can be from a minimum of three minutes to a maximum of twenty minutes. In championships, as a rule, preliminary rounds are limited to six minutes, with ten-minute semi-finals and a twenty-minute final. From which it will be clear that considerable physical fitness is a prerequisite for all contestants who hope to stand the pace.

The deciding point can be awarded for:

1. a throw which is made with some force and impetus and lands the opponent on his back;
2. a hold-down—when the opponent is held under control on his back and the control is maintained for thirty seconds;
3. a submission obtained from a choke or strangle lock or from a lock on the elbow;

4. scoring two near points (*waza-ari*)—for retaining a hold-down for more than twenty-five seconds but less than thirty seconds, or for a throwing technique which does not merit *ippon* but is sufficiently good to be worth between 80 per cent and 99 per cent of a point.

Should no point be scored in the time laid down, the judges and referee award the contest on the basis of near points or superior general skill and technique.

The contest over, the contestants tidy their jackets and stand in their original places, about twelve feet apart. When the referee has indicated the winner, the contestants bow to each other and then to the guests of honour before they leave the mat.

Whatever else it may do, the ceremonial certainly creates an atmosphere—and even the judoman at the peak of physical condition and highly confident of his chances might find it just a little unnerving.

Posture

To approach any competitive sport with a hazy or mistaken notion of your own intention can hardly be expected to produce successful results and may even prove to be your undoing. And this is no less true of contest judo than any other sport.

Many believe, for instance, that contest judo differs from *randori* in that the main object of the contestant is to avoid being defeated. That is to say, he may take measures to win—but only after he is sure he has eliminated any possibility of defeat. In consequence of this belief, many contest judomen tend to adopt an over-defensive posture with deeply-bent knees, body crouched, and arms stiff. This is quite wrong.

The simple truth is, there is no special "contest" posture—and any attempt to create one is likely to make things more difficult for you than for your opponent. A rigid stance that holds your opponent at arm's length may make it far from easy for him to throw you: but it will make it almost impossible for you to throw him.

As is taught in *randori*, the correct posture for contest judo is a relaxed one. For although there is a greater chance of your being thrown when you are relaxed, this is more than offset by the possible frequency, efficiency and power of your own throws.

It is largely a matter of confidence born of experience. To turn away from an opponent with the body completely relaxed in the course of an important contest calls for considerable confidence—and only contest experience will give that confidence. The determination to resist a throw to the last gasp, which one so often encounters in *shiai*, can be overdone. It is sometimes necessary to allow an opponent to commence a good technique in order to bring off an even better counter yourself.

Technique

Speed of thought and action is the keynote, and the greatest speed is achieved when the number of movements is fewest. Every unnecessary movement costs something in time and is therefore to be avoided. Take, for example, *Harai-goshi*, comprising three fast movements: step in with the right foot, turn on the left, sweep with the right hip and leg. How can this be speeded up? One way would be to manoeuvre yourself so that it is only necessary to step back with the left leg and then sweep with the right, so saving a precious moment. Even more time can be saved by the judoman of longer experience who manoeuvres himself so that he can pivot on his left foot and reap with his right in a single movement. Thus he will have whittled three movements down to one, giving his opponent a minimum of time to escape and virtually no time at all to counter.

This should be borne in mind whenever in this text I mention stepping in for a throw. I have included this movement because it is generally used in teaching judo; but the experienced judoman will know that in the heat and speed of a contest the step in will be dispensed with.

Tactics

These must vary with the individuals concerned, dependent upon relative heights, weights, speed, and so on. One general piece of advice, however, is that you should always try to dictate the speed at which a contest is fought. Quite obviously, your chances of success will be far greater if the contest is conducted at the speed you favour rather than that best suited to your opponent.

Teaching Judo

Because of the ever-increasing number of new enthusiasts who are eager for expert tuition, most contest men—whether they wish it or not—find themselves sooner or later called upon to teach. They should accept this situation as a privilege rather than a chore and do the job to the very best of their ability. No aspect of basic teaching should be overlooked or ignored—and this applies particularly to groundwork, which many judomen who should know better seem to think can be left to take care of itself. As a result of this attitude, it is not uncommon in club contests (and even occasionally in some international events) to see a contestant actually thrashing about like a stranded fish while being held down. In a grading examination contest, such a spectacle must tilt the examiners' decision adversely. And from the point of view of the contestant, it is futile.

In every judoman's experience there comes a time when he apparently goes stale and seems to make no progress at all. It is then that the knowledgeable instructor will turn his pupil's attention to a renewed study and practice of groundwork—reminding him of the too-often-forgotten fact that the principles he applies on the ground are identical to those he applies in his standing work.

The object of the teacher is twofold. Firstly, he must make his pupil understand the principle of a movement—that is, *why* it is made. And secondly, he must teach him to perform it. The former, which is by far the more important, is unfortunately often overlooked. This may be because the execution of a throw or ground movement can be sufficiently well mastered to pass an examiner even when the underlying principles are not fully understood. Good enough—but only up to a point. Beyond that point there can be no great progress without a thorough understanding of the principles. It is better, in fact, that a pupil should know unquestioningly what he is trying to do and why—even though success in performance eludes him—than that he should produce a reasonable facsimile in blind, unreasoning imitation.

An instructor must seek to establish the confidence of his pupils in himself and also nurture their own self-confidence. He must build on their knowledge step by step—never going too fast for the slowest of them or too slowly for those who progress quickly. Whenever possible, he should avoid pairing the older and less active with the young and vigorous; and, in mixed classes, he must ensure that the ladies are given a fair opportunity.

Finally, an instructor must always keep an eye open for the odd-man-out who invariably crops up in most group activities. He is usually a rather withdrawn fellow who, left to himself, seems always to be the one without a partner. The good instructor will take such a pupil unobtrusively under his wing, ensuring that he fully participates in all that is going on.

CHAPTER II

Movement and Tactics

Development of Maximum Power

Although "maximum effect—minimum effort" is a maxim which is familiar to all judomen, comparatively few really know how it should be applied. To achieve it, it is essential to keep the levers used against an opponent as near to your central point as possible. In other words, the arms and legs should be kept close to the body in order that the whole power of the body can be brought into use. Power will be weakened considerably if the legs and arms are stretched out too far. Figures 1 and 2 illustrate this.

In Figure 1, Uke is being pulled in the correct direction by Tori's left arm: but Tori's arm is stretched well away from his body, with the result that much of the pull has to be transmitted from the body along too long a lever, thereby lessening its power. Additionally, Uke's counter movement will be applied against Tori's arm which, without maximum power, will not be strong enough to maintain its pull. Consequently, Tori's attempted throw will fail.

FIG 1

In Figure 2, Tori's left arm is closer in to his body, with the result that the pull he exerts is more powerful and better able to resist counter action by Uke.

The same principle applies in groundwork. Concentration of body power is attained by keeping the body compact, with the legs drawn up, head tucked in, and elbows well in to the sides (Fig. 3). From this position it is possible to bridge the body (Fig. 4) and use the hips to manoeuvre (Fig. 5). Keeping the arms close to the body transmits the body power direct to the opponent. If you use your arms carelessly during groundwork, don't be surprised if you end up in an armlock.

FIG 2

FIG 3

FIG 4

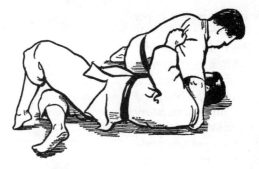

FIG 5

Attacking Against the Strength of an Opponent's Arms

To the Opponent's Front

Any number of frontal attacks can be checked with a straight, stiff arm. The arm is at its strongest when pointed directly at an opponent and to attack into it is futile. A sideways attack is, however, a very different matter. Strong as it is when met head on, the straight, stiff arm cannot easily resist an attack from the side (Fig. 6) or from below (Fig. 7).

FIG 6

FIG 7

To attack in this way it is not necessary to move in directly from either the right or the left. Attempting a throw to an opponent's front, the sideways attack is made by the turn of the body and lowering of the hips preparatory to an upward move against the arms. An application of this could be seen in, say, an attempted *Tai-otoshi* where the attack is made in the usual way and Uke straightens his arms. If Tori meets the straight arms head on, his movement comes to a dead stop. What he should do instead is attack, lifting his opponent slightly so that his attack is directed a little upwards (Fig. 8). Then, as Tori meets the resistance of Uke's arms, he begins his turn and moves sideways against Uke's arms, pushing them to Uke's right and thus removing the main source of resistance.

FIG 8

To the Opponent's Rear

Here the problem is even greater, because as Tori moves in he tends to meet Uke's arms head on. A typical example is *O-soto-gari*. Tori attacks and steps straight into a stiffened right arm, finding himself relatively in the position of an attacking boxer who is kept at bay by a series of straight jabs from his opponent. To continue would result in his pressure against Uke's arm driving Uke backwards, making the attack futile (Fig. 9).

To overcome this, Tori should pull Uke's right arm upwards and outwards, thereby greatly lessening his resistance (Fig. 10).

for getting in; once in pull down to create standing leg.
left arm pulls down, right arm moves head of opp. in backward/sideways movemen
CHIN DOWN.

FIG 9

FIG 10

Turning for a Throw to an Opponent's Front

An ill-judged turn can be of considerable benefit to an opponent. If Tori turns insufficiently and finishes with his own body in the way of Uke's fall, then, obviously, his attempted throw becomes impossible of achievement. In *Tai-otoshi*, for instance, an insufficient turn by Tori enables Uke to brace his right knee against Tori's right leg (Fig. 11) and prevent the throw. A greater turn by Tori would remove the possibility of this form of defence. Once in this situation, however, Tori can counteract it by bending his left knee more, which would automatically lower his right leg and so remove the source of Uke's defence.

FIG 11

Turning With the Hips

If you move your left hip back, your left leg will follow in the same curve. But the converse does not apply. Move your left leg back and the hip does not follow without conscious effort—making two movements where one would do. Furthermore, if you start a turn by moving your left leg back, you will find that the left leg passes behind the right leg at a fair distance from it (Fig. 12) and only about a three-quarters turn can be made before the hips lock and stop the movement.

If, instead, you commence the movement with the hip, the left leg passes close behind the right and the turn made is much greater (Fig. 13). The body is more compact as the turn is made and comes in closer to your opponent, lessening the danger of a counter move and putting you in a stronger position to make an effective throw.

A common mistake is to turn by pivoting the hips on a central point. Pushing the right hip forward and taking the left hip back does not make an effective turn. A throw attempted in this way is easy to stop and, if persisted in, easy to counter because a turn of this sort does not take you out of your opponent's line of approach.

The correct method would be to position the right hip and pivot round it, rather in the manner of describing a circle with a compass (Fig. 14). If the compass point is allowed to shift, the circle being drawn round a fixed point is broken. And so it is in judo. Your circular turn is broken just as soon as you change the position of your hip, thus opening you up to a counter.

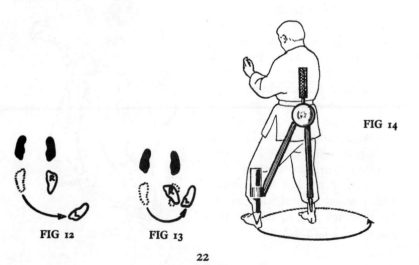

FIG 14

FIG 12   FIG 13

22

Positioning for the Throw

Ideal positioning is dependent upon the nature of the throw and also the individual physique and speed of each of the contestants. The object is, however, always the same—to effect a throw with the greatest speed and least effort.

When using the *Uchikomi* or *Butsukari* method of training, the initial step in is made for the sole purpose of getting into position to perform the throwing technique and it is the first of three movements: step in, turn, throw. Figure 15 shows the three steps for *Tai-otoshi*. In a contest there is no time for this, no matter how smooth the technique. It is therefore up to a contestant to manoeuvre his opponent into such a position that the first and possibly the second movement can be dispensed with. Not an easy task—but not impossible. It can be done by using what is known in judo as a "combination" technique. This, quite simply, is using the threat of one throw to force your opponent into a suitable position for the one you really intend to use. It calls for quick thinking and quick movement—but that, after all, is what judo is all about.

To avoid stepping in is not always possible, especially when attempting a throw to an opponent's rear, and there remains the danger of moving so close to your opponent that you have insufficient space to make the actual throw. In *O-soto-gari*, for instance, Tori might well

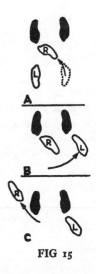

FIG 15

FIG 16

get so close to Uke that he is unable to bring his right hip through and between them in order to make the throw. The approach must be judged to allow for this movement (Fig. 16). There are other ways in which a bad step in can work to a contestant's disadvantage. If, in attempting *O-soto-gari*, Tori is too close to Uke (Fig. 17), there is the chance that he will not be able to bring his hip and leg past Uke and into position for the reap. From his opening stance (Fig. 18A) he must have sufficient space to bring his hip and leg through (Fig. 18B) to complete the throw (Fig. 18C): enough room, in fact, to turn without making contact with Uke's body until he needs to do so.

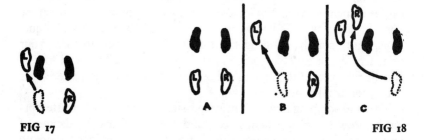

FIG 17   FIG 18

Economy of Movement

"Maximum effect—minimum effort" recurs constantly throughout judo training, and no apology is made for referring to it again. It cannot be too strongly stressed.

Synonymous with "minimum effort" is "economy of movement", and immediately apparent is the importance of never taking three steps where two will serve. And if the two steps can be reduced to one, so much the better. The throw will be even more effective.

A typical example is the final hip and leg movement in *Tai-otoshi*. If Tori turns to the left and thrusts back his right leg, he is making two movements—uneconomic in time and inefficient in effect. But if as he completes the drawing back of his left hip he projects his right hip, which will take his right leg with it, into position for the throw, he will be making only one movement.

This technique can be used for several throws.

Position of the Hips

The position of the hips in relation to the position of an opponent is of great significance. All power and control should emanate from hip movement and it is therefore essential to move with the hips square to the line of advance.

Figure 19 shows Tori standing relaxed, facing Uke and holding his jacket with the normal grip, his hips square to his front. If Tori now steps forward with his right foot, he must guard against instinctively advancing his right hip with it. For although this is normal enough in walking, it must not be done in judo. Figure 20 shows the correct movement.

FIG 19

FIG 20

FIG 21

An attempted throw with the hip advanced (Fig. 21) will be lacking a large proportion of power, and the amount of power lost can be equated to the distance by which the hip has been moved from its correct position.

Since the power for an attack comes from the hips, the bigger the turn made with them the greater the power.

Remember, then: hips square to the line of advance.

Economy of Effort

A throw which is successful against an opponent weighing ten or eleven stone can only be regarded as completely satisfactory if it can also be applied with equal success against one weighing fifteen or sixteen stone. This might seem formidable indeed when considered in application to a throw which entails lifting one's opponent. Yet it can be done—and without any superhuman exertion.

In throws of the *Seoi-nage* type there is a natural inclination to drive into an opponent and overcome his resistance by attempting to lift him bodily from the mat. And in an attempted throw of the *O-goshi* type it is not uncommon for Tori to complete his turn and then drive his hips back and upwards into Uke, thus sweeping him completely off the mat. All very well if Uke is of a fairly light build, but not so good if he is a heavyweight. Once the full weight of a heavy body is taken it is no longer possible to continue the turn—and if the throw is not successful at that stage it cannot be taken any further.

If these forms of bodily lifting are not the right answer, then what is? Let us take a look at what happens in weight lifting. One can often see weights lifted which it would be impossible to raise in the form of pressing a dead weight. What happens is, upward pressure is exerted and the lifter drops his body below the bar, achieving his position without undertaking the fearful exertion of the press. And this is precisely what is done in judo to lift an opponent of any weight. Tori pushes Uke's arms upwards to prevent him holding out. Then, by relaxing and bending the knees as he turns, he drops below Uke's weight. A final thrust back will sweep Uke from the mat without great physical effort on the part of Tori.

The importance of having the hip and leg in the right direction and position for a throw involving a sweep or reap—such as *Harai-goshi* or

O-soto-gari—should not be underestimated. A division of power in any sphere must mean a lessening of efficiency. If the power of a throw has to be divided between lift and drive in the true direction then, clearly, the throw must be less effective than one in which all the power is already concentrated in the correct direction. The sweep should, of course, be made low—for the higher the sweep the more effort has to go into lift. This becomes self-evident in practice, where it is seen that lift has to be exerted to the level at which contact with an opponent is made. In *Harai-goshi*, for example, if Tori makes contact with Uke's leg just below the knee, it is only necessary for him to exert lift to overcome the twelve or fifteen inches between the mat and that point. But if Tori's leg is thrust across to make contact with Uke at hip level, lift will have to be exerted to that point—perhaps three or four feet.

Generally, the reap or sweep must be made directly backwards. Should it be made upwards, Tori's leg would slide up Uke's body—not only giving Uke time to escape or counter but also failing to make contact until it is far too high up Uke's body to be effective.

Power for the reap must come from the hips. The leg is only the reaping instrument and generates little power of its own.

Direction of Attack

Attack must be aimed in the direction in which the opponent's balance is at its weakest. In the heat and speed of a contest, however, in which the relative positions of Tori and Uke are constantly changing, it is not at all easy to decide which that direction is.

As a rule, balance is weak directly to the front and rear when, with neither a foot nor a hip advanced, a person is in the normal standing position (Fig. 22). The line of attack in this stance is clearly shown in Figure 23.

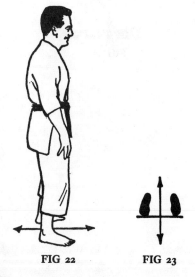

FIG 22   FIG 23

27

If Tori delivers his attack in this direction, Uke is unable to defend himself in the popular way by bending his knees, pressing the advanced foot against the mat and bracing himself (Fig. 24). Instead, he should move his hips so that Tori's line of attack is no longer the correct one. Figure 25 illustrates this, with Tori attacking with, say, *Tai-otoshi* to Uke's front. In defence, Uke moves his left hip and foot forward, naturally adjusting his balance as he does so. The result is that Tori is now attacking in the wrong direction and may well fail (Fig. 26).

DIRECTION OF RESISTANCE   DIRECTION OF PULL

FIG 24

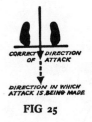

CORRECT DIRECTION OF ATTACK

DIRECTION IN WHICH ATTACK IS BEING MADE

FIG 25

CORRECT DIRECTION OF ATTACK   DIRECTION IN WHICH ATTACK IS BEING MADE

FIG 26

CHAPTER III

Use of the Arms

Throws to an Opponent's Front

Figure 27 shows Tori in a normal upright stance with his arms held in front of him at chest level and his fists together, so that his arms form a circle. To hold Uke, it is only necessary for him to part his arms a little and grasp Uke's jacket in the customary way (Fig. 28), his arms still forming a circle in front of him. If, as he turned, Tori could keep his arms and opponent in this position and maintain his balance and control, he would not have to consider the problem of breaking Uke's balance. It would be broken automatically (Fig. 29).

FIG 27

FIG 28

FIG 29

FIG 30

In practice, however, the combination of Uke's weight and his evasive action prevents Tori from maintaining the ideal position of his arms in relation to his body. To restore this, Tori must increase his turn, driving his hips back into Uke. The following example illustrates this.

Tori attempts *Tai-otoshi*, but Uke resists and succeeds in transferring his balance a little to his left. In meeting the additional resistance, Tori leaves his arms a little behind the ideal position (Fig. 30). Because of this, and although the turn has been made, Uke manages to retain his balance sufficiently to avoid being thrown. But if Tori maintains his pull to Uke's front he can still make his throw by driving his left hip further back, thus restoring the relative position of his arms to his body (Fig. 31).

FIG 31

In throws of the *Seoi-nage* type, Tori may have to lower h
by bending his knees in order to drive his hips back into U
requires complete relaxation.

Unexpected resistance accounts for what is probably t
common of arm faults—that of raising the elbow above should
It should be remembered that the higher the elbow is lifted al
level the greater the loss of power, but eagerness to comple
only too often outweighs common sense. The sort of thing that
is this: Tori attempts a throw such as *Seoi-nage* and allows Uk
out by stiffening his arms, with the result that Tori's tu
to a complete stop long before Uke is in any danger (Fig. 32)
tinue to turn in the same arc is impossible and Tori's real an
change the position or technique. Tori, however, decides to
seems a far easier course. He raises his right elbow when h
checked and is then able to continue the turn to its conclusion
Unfortunately, continuing the turn in this way has absolutel
on Uke—and Tori only succeeds in turning his back on an
who is still on balance. A fatal mistake.

That the elbow should always be kept below shoulder le
be over-emphasised. It is as important at the end of a throv

FIG 32   FIG 33

the beginning. The commencing lift which breaks an opponent's balance should be maintained throughout the throw. Admittedly, it is often difficult during a throw to be certain whether or not lift is being applied at any particular point; and it might seem that by raising the right elbow the opponent is being lifted. But, as Figure 33 shows, this is not so. On the contrary, the raising of the elbow forces the forearm downwards, pressing Uke down and making it that much harder to sweep him from the mat. Consequently, it is most unlikely that the throw could be successful.

The upward lift must be maintained throughout, and Figure 34 illustrates the lift at the end of the throw in *Tai-otoshi*. As well as lifting, every effort should be made to pull the opponent directly to *his* front when attempting a throw in that direction.

With a throw such as *O-goshi*, it will be found that Uke frequently escapes by sliding round Tori's right hip (Fig. 35). Tori may himself be to blame for this through misuse of his arms. As he attacks, Tori must pull evenly with both arms to Uke's front and a little upwards. If the pull is greater with Tori's left arm, Uke will advance his right side and will tend to move round Tori's hip. Alternatively, if Tori pulls

FIG 34

FIG 35

harder with his right arm he will bring Uke's left hip forward, thereby changing his correct line of attack to Uke's left (Fig. 36) and, because of the far greater turn entailed, making the throw much more difficult. In addition, this unbalanced pull with the right arm might bring Tori's right side close to Uke, making it easier for Uke to check the throw with his left arm or hip. Figure 36 shows Uke too far over to Tori's left—more open, perhaps, to *Koshi-guruma*. Some experienced contest men would use a pull slightly to Uke's left in order to straighten his body and prevent him from moving to his right. Variation of the pull is always admissible provided the judoman knows what he is doing and why.

FIG 36

FIG 37

FIG 38

33

It is not so difficult to maintain the pull to the front with the left hand; but the right hand is inclined to push away or straighten, increasing the radius of the circle and pushing Uke round Tori's right hip. If this happens, Tori is actually helping Uke to escape the throw (Fig. 37). In the case of *Tai-otoshi*, Uke would step over Tori's attacking right leg. But when the turn is made correctly, Tori's pull with his right hand becomes a push to Uke's front quite early in the turn (Fig. 38). This movement drives Uke straight to his front and over Tori's hip or leg.

Throws to an Opponent's Rear

When making a throw to the rear, an experienced judoman might avoid his opponent's defensive arm by making his attempt from arm's length. In Figure 39, this method is being employed for *O-soto-gari*. Its disadvantage is that it provides Tori with little control over Uke; and, having obtained this position, Tori will find the throw still very difficult to accomplish. Furthermore, he may well open himself to a counter throw.

It is just as necessary for Tori to get close to Uke for rear throws as it is for throws to Uke's front.

Using the "chest expander" method of breaking balance, Tori can operate almost as if attempting a throw to Uke's front. Just as if using spring exercisers, Tori pulls forward, outward and a little upward (Fig. 40). Uke may react by resisting away to his rear—which helps Tori—but he is not allowed by Tori to move back-

FIG 39

wards. The pull is all-important. Its upward direction lifts Uke, making it easier to cope with his weight, while the forward direction prevents his escape by stepping backwards. The outward direction takes Uke's arms sideways, where they are considerably weaker.

Applying this to a particular throw, in this case *O-soto-gari*, Tori maintains the initial pull, its outward direction permitting him to move in between Uke's arms and come in really close so that in the final phase of the throw he can bring the whole power of his body into action against Uke (Fig. 40).

The important thing is to get in close.

FIG 40

Variations in the Use of the Arms

Particularly in throws to Uke's front, Tori must vary the use of his arms according to the difference in height between himself and Uke. If Tori is the taller, he can lift Uke from above; but if Uke is the taller, Tori must push upwards from below.

As well as lifting Uke, Tori must also pull him towards his front in order to destroy his balance. There is one method of doing this which employs the wrists as well as the arms—the wrists and forearms shaping like the neck of a swan. It is applied as follows.

If Uke is the taller, Tori turns his wrists in towards himself and thrusts Uke upwards (Fig. 41). If Tori is the taller, he turns his wrists outwards, away from himself, in a lifting motion (Fig. 42). In either case it is a graceful but difficult movement—effective in theory but liable to break down under contest conditions with a strong and experienced opponent . . . unless Tori has very great skill.

The "chest expander" technique, already briefly mentioned, is also subject to variations in the use of the arms. Timed correctly,

FIG 41

FIG 42

it is a powerful and effective method of overcoming a resisting opponent and basically it consists of Tori pulling Uke to his front and a little upwards. Tori brings his elbows outwards, lifting at the same time with his wrists (Fig. 43). In all circumstances, the initial attack is made in the way just described. It is then that the variations come into play.

Should Tori be the taller, the pull is made with the wrists turned so that the palms of his hands face downwards (Fig. 43). As the pull reaches its conclusion, the wrists tend to turn inwards (Fig. 44). Tori continues his pull to Uke's front as he turns, and his pull with the right hand becomes a push as the turn progresses.

FIG 43

If Tori is shorter than Uke, he makes the normal initial approach, reaching the position shown in Figure 43, and then turns his wrists so that the palms of his hands are towards himself. As he turns, continuing his pull to Uke's front, Tori's arms drive upwards. This method is an ideal entry for such throws as *Seoi-nage* and *Tsurikomi-goshi*.

FIG 44

Use of the Right Arm

The correct use of the right arm in a throw is every bit as important as the correct use of the left. Being the pulling arm in a right-handed throw, the left arm can be used effectively even if the maximum possible power is not obtained. The right, however, not only loses its effectiveness if not used correctly but can even get in Tori's own way, preventing the throw.

When the initial pull is made, Tori's elbows are pulled back, as shown in Figure 43. If this position is maintained, as it ought to be, then all should go well. The pull has brought Uke close; and as Tori turns, his right arm is in the ideal position to obtain maximum leverage. It is a common fault, however, for Tori to increase the radius of his circle by straightening his right arm as he turns. The result is that when he reaches the climax of his throw Tori finds that he has his elbow tucked between Uke and himself, making it impossible to obtain the close contact required—and losing his free and comfortable posture into the bargain. It is therefore essential that the right elbow should remain at its usual level throughout.

Extra Drive from the Arms

Once the arms have been used to break an opponent's balance

37

in the early stages of a throw, they should thereafter retain their relative position to the body. There must be synchronisation between the arms and the body, and any attempt to throw with the arms alone is doomed to failure. With experience, though, one comes to know when extra drive from the arms or a change of direction might make all the difference between failure and success.

To gain this experience, it is imperative to take part in hard *randori* with people you can throw—even if, in return, you are thrown at times. The object is to get so used to the feel of actually making a throw that at at any stage of it you can judge how close you are to final success.

Let us now look at a situation where extra drive from the arms could save the day. Tori is attempting *Ippon-seoi-nage*. As he turns, Uke "sticks" and just manages to check Tori's movement (Fig. 45). Tori must now come out of his throw fast or get it on its way once more. If he is to continue, Tori must regain the free movement of his hips. To do this, he bends his left knee a little and drops his right leg back past the outside of Uke's right leg (Fig. 46). This brings Tori back under Uke in a position in which he can again move his hips. He now turns a little to his left and drives Uke forward to his front and upward with his arms—and, with the extra drive, should be able to complete his throw (Fig. 47).

The arms can be used to increase the radius of the circle in which Tori is attempting to take Uke. In *Tai-otoshi*, for instance, Uke may well manage to get close to Tori and brace himself against Tori's

FIG 45

FIG 46

leg (Fig. 48). If Tori persists, he is only pulling Uke against his own leg and defeating himself. Instead, to complete the throw it is only necessary for Tori to widen the circle, so that Uke is pivoted round Tori's outstretched leg and not over it (Fig. 49). To do this, Tori has only to straighten his right arm and then drive Uke round him.

FIG 47

FIG 48

FIG 49

Changing Direction

The arms can be used with the body to completely change the direction of a throw as an opponent resists, so that he is thrown in the direction in which he is pulling or resisting.

When such a manoeuvre is necessary should be self-evident. It would clearly be pointless to persist in attempting to throw an opponent to his front when that opponent has succeeded in recovering his balance and is throwing all his weight to his rear. The obvious thing to do is change the direction of the throw to the opponent's rear. Tori must at all times be able to follow Uke's movements and change his own to take advantage of them.

The illustrations show Tori changing from an attempted *Ashi-guruma* to Uke's front (Fig. 50) to *O-soto-gari* to his rear (Fig. 51).

Variations of throw which can be used by following an opponent's defensive movements are limitless. Any imaginative and flexible judo-man can develop them by working slowly with a co-operative partner.

FIG 50   FIG 51

CHAPTER IV

Use of Full Body Power and Weight

Drive from the Hips

In his basic training, the judoman is taught to continue his turn. He usually does so by pivoting on his left foot, so that the whole body turns in one piece. This is correct judo—but the turn can be made far more powerful and effective if the final drive is made with the hips. See what a difference it makes in a throw such as *Tai-otoshi*, where Tori has reached what might be called the final stage (Fig. 52). As Uke's position is now critical, he may be expected to put up considerable resistance to avoid losing a contest point. It is therefore necessary for Tori to put all that he has into completing the throw. So he con-

FIG 52

FIG 53

tinues the turn to his left and, without a break in his movement or rhythm, drives his left hip back as far as he can. At the same time, he drives Uke direct to his, Uke's, front with his arms (Fig. 53). This combined action of hip and arms almost hammers Uke into the mat.

A variation used by experienced contest men is to make the turn for throws such as *Tai-otoshi* with the hips pushed forward (Fig. 54). There is a serious danger here of being countered if Uke's balance is not broken as Tori turns; but if Uke's balance has been broken, Tori completes the throw by driving his hips back. Because of the far greater arc through which the hips move in this backward drive (Fig. 55), the throw is made with correspondingly more impetus.

FIG 54

FIG 55

Body Posture and Control

A main cause of failure when attempting a throw is the collapse or bend of the body at the waist, often the result of getting too far away from an opponent. Perhaps Uke pushes Tori away as he turns and, in order to re-establish contact, Tori bends forward at the hips into the position shown in Figure 56. He does in fact make contact at hip level—but the move has no effect on Uke, who will be in no

FIG 56

FIG 57

danger from the attempted throw.

The same fault could be attributable to an insufficient turn at the last stage of a throw—possibly through failure to turn the left foot enough to the left (Fig. 57). When, because of this mistake, the turn is automatically halted, it might seem the natural thing to do to bend at the waist in order to complete the throw—but the effort will prove fruitless.

Figure 58 shows Tori attempting *Tai-otoshi*. He has reached the final stage of his throw and has met strong resistance from Uke, who has thrown his weight back to his rear. To overcome this, Tori has attempted to bring strength into play rather than skill. Instead of turning and driving his left hip back, he has

FIG 58

43

tried to drive Uke to his, Uke's, front with his arms and has doubled himself up at the waist. But although Tori has brought his hips closer to Uke, he has not disturbed Uke's defensive position at all.

Compare Tori's posture in Figure 58 with the one he maintains in Figure 59. In the latter he has kept his body upright, countering Uke's resistance by continuing to drive him to his front. At the same time, he is driving his left hip back, achieving his object of completely destroying Uke's balance. This is the right way of going about it, with a good posture and the body properly controlled.

FIG 59

Attacking Side of the Body

In judo one hears about keeping the body upright, but what this really means is that the side of the body which attacks the opponent must be kept straight.

When Tori attempts *Tsurikomi-ashi*, for example, the attack is made with the left leg and side (Fig. 60). The dotted line in the illustration indicates the straightness of the left side of Tori's body which has to be maintained to achieve maximum power. Similarly, Figure 61 demonstrates how the same side of the body should be kept straight for an attempted *De-ashi-barai*.

Figure 62 shows Tori attacking in *O-soto-gari*. Note that this throw is made from the hip, not just the leg, and that he develops his power by keeping the entire right side of his body straight—even down to his toes.

It is the leg upon which Tori stands (the right leg in Figures 60 and 61, the left in Figure 62) that is generally kept bent in order to lower the hip and improve the balance and also increase the extent of reach with the other leg and hip.

44

FIG 60

FIG 61

FIG 62

The Back

From the foregoing it will be obvious that the back has to be kept straight in all throws. A crouched, doubled-up posture congests the hips, preventing turn and freedom of movement.

Defensive Postures

Successful defence is just as dependent upon maximum body power as is successful attack. Every defensive move should be made with the idea of a possible counter attack in mind: but the more defensive one's position becomes the less chance there is of countering. It is important, therefore, even in defence to maintain a good posture. For although bending at the waist and crouching might seem the easiest way of resisting a throw, it is certainly not the surest way. The consequent restriction of movement and loss of body power make it anything but a safe defence against a competent judo-man.

Holding an Opponent's Jacket

There is no fixed or regulation hold on an opponent's jacket. The time-honoured hold of right hand on his left lapel and left hand on his right sleeve just below the elbow is still by far the most common— but there are many variations, each with its advantages and weaknesses. Of this basic hold, the main advantage is that one gains great leverage or pull on the right sleeve and considerable drive from the right hand on the left lapel. Its weakness lies in the fact that it must almost always be changed if Tori wishes to attempt a left-hand technique—and the change usually gives Uke sufficient warning to escape or counter the attack.

A change may be necessary to obtain more leverage and lift on an opponent, effected perhaps by holding his collar at the back of the neck with the right hand. But there is danger in such a high hold, for it gives an opportunity

FIG 63

to the opponent to attack under the arms. This apart, in such a hold Tori will find that his forearm lies along the back of Uke's neck, parallel with his own chest, thus making the power of his pull come from the forearm working sideways—not lengthwise, as it should. It often happens that the muscles of the forearm are unable to stand the strain of the sideways pull and a very sore spot develops deep in the arm, just below the elbow. This hold can be seen in Figure 63, in which the arrow shows the angle at which the right arm exerts its pull.

Holding an opponent's jacket at the armpits with both hands is a variation which provides a grip sufficiently high to give lift, sufficiently wide to give leverage or pull, but not so wide that it weakens defence. It should, however, be used with discretion. There is no point in Tori attempting it if Uke is so much taller as to make the hold uncomfortably high. And, all else being equal, there is the disadvantage of there being no free material at the armpits to allow Tori any play on the jacket, should it be required. An alternative is to hold Uke's sleeves fairly near the ends. But although this gives a tremendously effective pull it is very weak defensively, allowing Uke the opportunity of slipping easily between Tori's arms.

Widely used is the variation in which Tori holds both of Uke's lapels. It provides ample lift and has the added advantage of being very strong in defence, Tori's hold being so close to the centre of Uke's body that Uke has great difficulty in turning to attack. On the debit side, and paradoxically, the closeness of both hands to the centre of Uke's body makes it hard for Tori to obtain effective control over Uke.

In the final analysis, naturally enough, each judoman must decide for himself which hold he intends to use: and only individual experience will really produce the answer to the problems presented by each hold.

Using the Hold to Maximum Effect

Once having decided upon his hold, Tori must make maximum use of it to ensure that even his slightest movement will immediately affect Uke. This is essential, and it is achieved by Tori letting his hands drop by means of their own weight to the fullest extent allowed by the hold without dropping the elbows, which must be kept out at the usual angle. At this point, when his hold on Uke's jacket prevents Tori's hands from dropping any lower, Tori's wrists should be turned inwards, quite naturally and without force. Tori will then find that he has a firm and effective hold on Uke's jacket without having expended any energy—a hold which allows no slack on Uke's jacket and one which instantly transmits any movement by Tori to Uke's body.

Direction of Movement: The Circle in Judo

Effective judo movements are almost always circular in direction. Tori pulls in a circle and also moves Uke in a circle—although not always the same one.

An example of this is *Tsurikomi-ashi*. Tori turns to his left and pulls with his left arm in a circle which follows the arc described by his own left hip as it withdraws. His right arm follows his left in the same arc. He is therefore making a circle to his left. The effect of this on Uke is to turn him in a quite different circle. Tori's pull as he turns brings Uke to his own front, and the act of turning makes Tori's right hand pull become a push or drive to Uke's front. If Tori has lifted as he pulled, Uke will be off balance and pulled to his front, where the action is completed by Tori blocking Uke's right foot with his left foot and turning Uke in a circle to his front. Figure 64 shows the different arcs in which Tori and Uke turn.

Another situation in which the circular direction of movement can be clearly seen occurs in a throw such as *Ko-uchi-gari*. Tori lifts Uke and, by describing a clockwise circle with his left foot, brings the sole of his left foot behind Uke's left heel. As soon as sufficiently close contact with Uke's body is obtained, the initial forward and upward pull of Tori's arms is changed. His hands now move in a circle, first towards himself and upwards and then over and away towards Uke's rear. The foot and hand movements thus far are illustrated in Figure 65. To complete the throw,

FIG 64

FIG 65

FIG 66

48

Tori's left hand continues its circle so that it pulls back past his own left side while his right hand continues its circle, driving against Uke's left shoulder. Tori's left foot continues its circle so that Uke's left foot is pulled forward (Fig. 66).

The continuance of circular movement is most important. If Tori's circle is broken, he will lose control of Uke and the throw—no matter which it is—will fail.

Use and Misuse of Lift

Lift, in judo, is a movement made by a continuation of arm (often wrist) and body movement. To attempt it in any way which entails taking the whole weight of an opponent's body is foolhardy. Yet it is a common enough mistake which causes many an attack to fail. An instance can be seen in Figure 67, where Tori is lifting Uke bodily off the mat and thereby taking his whole weight. Under this burden, Tori's hips are congested and the only way he can complete the throw is to bend forward at the waist and hurl Uke over his shoulder to the mat. And this means he must lift Uke even higher, at the expense of time and energy.

In a contest, the time element is vital. The more Uke is lifted the longer he has in which to escape or counter. In addition to which,

FIG 67

FIG 68

the pointlessness of dissipating energy on attempting a throw which is going to depend on strength alone should be self-evident.

If lift is correctly applied, it should be effective irrespective of the opponent's weight. Taking *Harai-goshi* as an example, Figure 68 shows the angles of pull and lift applied by Tori to bring Uke's weight forward on to his toes. The lift is maintained to the final stages of the throw, and it never necessitates the taking of Uke's full bodily weight. Remember, too, that in *Harai-goshi*—which means Sweeping Hip or Loin—the throw is a sweep made with Tori's own hip or loin and *not* a sweep against the hip or loin of Uke: a subtle but important difference.

To complete the throw, Tori turns and sweeps Uke's legs away with his hip movement. A misinterpretation of intention in the form of a sweep against Uke's hip could not help but be ineffectual—and if we follow the movements entailed we can see why. Tori would have to sweep upwards to attack Uke's hip, and his right leg would make contact with Uke's right leg at about knee level. It would then slide up to the region of Uke's waist, where further free upward movement would be prevented by Uke's bent posture (Fig. 69). Nevertheless, Tori could not make the throw without continuing the upward movement and sweeping Uke bodily over his own throwing leg or hip, which, under these circumstances, would call for considerable strength, effort and time.

The correct move is, therefore, for Tori to sweep *backwards* against Uke's leg, continuing his turn at the same time (Fig. 70). Tori's drive

FIG 69

FIG 70

with body and arms to Uke's front, coupled with his backwards sweep of hip and leg, will carry Uke over his outstretched leg, which makes contact with Uke's leg comparatively low (Fig. 71). Tori thus slides Uke off the mat instead of lifting him.

This principle applies to many throws—the lift and drive of the throwing technique sliding Uke from the mat rather than lifting him from it.

FIG 71

Use of the Chest

It is important at all times that the chest be free, both for proper breath control and the application of maximum power. To hunch the shoulders (Fig. 72) is to constrict the chest, with a consequent limit to freedom of movement and loss of efficiency.

The ideal is an upright posture, with chest expanded, back hollowed and shoulders back (Fig. 73). Assumed naturally, it affords free movement and relaxation. But don't try to force it. Any stance which requires conscious effort is taken at the inevitable cost of relaxation.

FIG 72

In Figure 74 Tori is applying *Tai-otoshi*, his "open" chest permitting freedom of movement and maximum leverage. With this posture he will extract the fullest possible effect from the throw.

FIG 73

FIG 74

Use of the Wrists

The full power of the body is transmitted to an opponent through the arms, but it is the curve of the wrists that dictates the direction in which that power is exerted. Incorrect use of the wrists can therefore nullify every other advantage.

Look at Figure 75, in which Tori is facing Uke and holding with his right wrist straight, his arm pointing directly through Uke's left shoulder. When he attempts to move Uke to his, Uke's, front by pushing to the left with his own right arm he is only

FIG 75

52

able to bring the power of his right arm, and perhaps his shoulder, into action against Uke.

Compare this with Figure 76, where Tori's wrist is turned in the direction in which he wishes to exert power. He can now use his hip to bring the full power of his body into play against Uke, the force flowing from the hip through the body, arm and wrist.

The correct use of the wrist in throws such as *Tai-otoshi* can be seen in Figure 77, while Figure 78 shows the direction it should take in rear throws like *O-soto-gari.*

FIG 76

FIG 77

FIG 78

In defence, too, the wrists can play a decisive part. Uke can effectively prevent Tori from obtaining the lift by the simple expedient of using his wrists correctly. All he has to do is turn his wrists downwards as he pushes Tori away by straightening his arms. Uke's full power will be transmitted through those downward-turned wrists—and if Tori persists against it he is liable to have his balance destroyed to his rear, with a counter following (Fig. 79).

To prevent Uke attacking, Tori may keep his right hand—which is holding Uke's left lapel—well over to Uke's centre with the wrist turned inwards and a little down. This makes it difficult for Uke to turn for a right-handed throw. For the same effect, Tori might find it advantageous to transfer his left-hand hold from Uke's sleeve to his lapel.

FIG 79

Further Attempts at a Throw

Provided Tori maintains his balance after the failure of an attack, there is no reason why a second attempt or even a series of attempts should not be made. To resume his attack, Tori must retain his forward and upward pull and readjust his position—usually by stepping back slightly. The power of the second or subsequent attacks should be increased.

Here, then, are the generalities that the contest judoman should know and keep well in mind. In the following chapters will be found the details of specific throws.

CHAPTER V

Ashi-Waza – Leg Techniques

In this chapter are included those throws which are effected by Tori's use of leg or foot but which do not entail close bodily contact.

TSURIKOMI-ASHI—DRAWING ANKLE THROW

Opportunity

When Uke has his balance forward and steps or is about to step forward with legs straight or only slightly bent.

Timing

As Uke is about to place his weight upon the forward foot—the one to be attacked.

The Throw

Assuming that Uke is moving forward with his right foot, Tori pivots to his left on his right foot, lifting and pulling Uke to his front. Bending his right knee, for balance and flexibility of movement, and keeping his left leg and the left side of his body in a straight line, Tori brings the sole of his left foot up against the base of Uke's right shin, as shown in Figure 80.

It is essential that Tori makes his throw by pivoting. Any forward movement, either of body or foot, will defeat his purpose by

FIG 80

55

rendering him unable to turn. He must bring Uke forward on to his outstretched left foot.

In making his initial lift and pull, Tori must bring his elbows back and keep them well up. His wrists should curve inward and upward. This, too, is shown in Figure 80. Additional power can be obtained by driving his hips forward as his foot makes contact with Uke's shin.

The entire movement is fast and brief.

Variations

If Tori is shorter than Uke

Tori must exert greater lift. A normal pull to Uke's front by a shorter man might pull Uke downwards. Tori might therefore, in starting the movement, lower his body and turn his wrists upwards. This produces a very powerful throw, developing tremendous upward thrust.

If Tori is taller than Uke

A straight pull to Uke's front will be sufficient. The necessary lift will result naturally from Tori's superior height. Tori can, in fact, allow his wrists to drop a little.

Successive Attack with the Same Throw

A common fault is Tori's failure to turn sufficiently, thus placing his own body in the line of Uke's movement. To redress this, Tori must hold Uke off balance while he replaces his left foot on the mat and steps back with his right foot, turning it more to his left as he does so. He then attacks again. Figure 81 shows (A) the faulty positioning of the feet for the first attempt, and (B) the correction made for the second attempt.

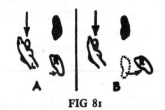

FIG 81

Change of Throw in the Same Direction

Tori may find himself being pushed away backwards as he attacks, making it difficult for him to continue with *Tsurikomi-ashi*. Obviously, it is better to abandon the attempt and try a different throw. Holding

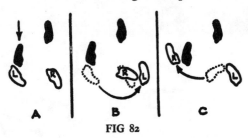

FIG 82

Uke off balance to his front by the lift and pull of his arms, Tori can pivot from his original stance (Fig. 82A) to his left on his right foot, until he is facing the same direction as Uke, replacing his left foot on the mat to the outside of Uke's left foot and as far back as he can reasonably manage (Fig. 82B). He must then thrust his right leg across Uke's front (Fig. 82C) to attack with *Tai-otoshi* (Fig. 83).

Should Uke escape *Tsurikomi-ashi* by stepping over Tori's left foot, Tori might continue with *Hiza-guruma* or, by moving his right leg round to Uke's left, with a side Sacrifice technique.

FIG 83

Change of Direction of Attack

It is necessary to follow Uke's movements as he attempts to avoid Tori's attack. A usual form of defence is for Uke to throw his weight backwards and to his left—exactly opposite to the direction in which Tori is attacking (Fig. 84). Tori uses his arms and wrists to hold Uke in this new position. Then, by pivoting to his right on his right foot, he might succeed with a left-handed *Tai-otoshi* (Fig. 85). Another possibility is *Osoto-gari* to the right (Fig. 86), which can be effected by Tori placing his left foot close to Uke's right and reaping with his right hip and leg.

57

FIG 84

FIG 85

Possible Counters to Tsurikomi-ashi

Uke can block the throw by bracing the leg being attacked—the right, say—on the mat and then pivoting to the left to counter with a left *Tai-otoshi* or a Sacrifice throw such as *Yoko-wakari* or *Yoko-sutemi*.

Alternatively, with Tori attacking Uke's right leg, Uke can step over the attacking leg and pivot on his right foot to his right and counter with a left *Tai-otoshi*.

Or Uke could step over Tori's attacking left leg and counter with *Hiza-guruma* against Tori's right leg.

FIG 86

DE-ASHI-BARAI—SWEEPING THE ADVANCING ANKLE

Opportunity

When Uke, moving fairly freely, moves his right foot in any forward direction.

Timing

As Uke is about to place his weight upon the foot to be attacked, or as the moving foot passes the other.

58

The Throw

If attacking Uke's right foot, Tori pivots slightly to his right on his right foot, breaking Uke's balance to his front with a forward and upward pull of the arms. Turning his left foot so that the sole makes contact with the outside of Uke's right ankle, Tori sweeps Uke's right leg away to Uke's left. Tori's sweeping leg is kept straight, in line with the left side of his body (Fig. 87). His left arm pulls to Uke's left and upwards, his right to Uke's right and upwards. Both wrists curve inwards. The movement can be compared with turning a big wheel to the left.

Instead of sweeping Uke's leg across, Tori might sweep it back against Uke's other leg. But in either event, Tori must sweep Uke's foot along the mat and not lift it upwards.

FIG 87

Variations

If Tori is shorter than Uke
The lift will be a thrust from below, with the wrists curved upwards.
If Tori is taller than Uke
He will be able to lift from above, with his wrists turned down a little.

In fact, differences in height between Tori and Uke have no appreciable effect on this throw.

Successive Attack with the Same Throw

It is not advised because of the opportunity it would give Uke to use the same throw on Tori as a counter.

Change of Throw in the Same Direction

When attacked with *De-ashi-barai*, Uke's usual reaction is to either whip back his right foot, so that Tori misses with his sweep, or plant his right foot firmly on the mat. Tori's choice of second throw will therefore depend upon the position in which he finds Uke. If Uke takes his right leg back, or resists with his right knee well bent, an attack with *Hiza-guruma* might succeed. Alternatively, if Uke advances his right foot, Tori could attack with *Tsurikomi-ashi*. In both cases Tori must move his right foot, turning it at the same time so that his toes are pointed to the left.

Tai-otoshi or *Harai-goshi* would become possible if Uke were to bring his balance forward.

Change of Direction of Attack

Uke, having stopped the throw by the simple expedient of being very firmly placed on his feet, should have retained his balance. Consequently, a change of direction will be difficult to achieve.

If Uke leans back, Tori can drive in for *O-uchi-gari* to the left (Fig. 88), or for *O-soto-gari*, attacking Uke's left leg. Or he might attack Uke's left leg with *Ko-uchi-gari* (Fig. 89).

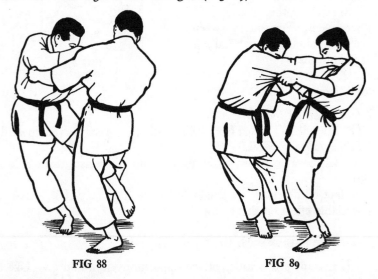

FIG 88   FIG 89

Should Uke avoid the throw by taking his right foot back, Tori can turn to his right to attack with *Tai-otoshi* to the left. He will have to change the direction of his arms and wrists as he does so, in order to drive Uke directly to his front as well as lifting him (as has been previously shown in Figure 85). Tori can obtain terrific drive from the turn of his hips and the straightening of his body.

Possible Counters to De-ashi-barai

Uke could take his right foot back to avoid the throw and then follow Tori's foot with it to apply *De-ashi-barai* against Tori's left foot.

He could, having avoided the sweep, replace his right foot on the mat and, by turning to his right, counter-attack with a left-handed *Tai-otoshi*.

Or, replacing his right foot on the mat, he could bring his left leg through to attack with a left-handed *O-soto-gari*.

Alternatively, instead of avoiding Tori's sweeping foot, Uke can place his right foot firmly on the mat to block the attack and then, with his left foot, attack with *Hiza-guruma*.

HIZA-GURUMA—KNEE WHEEL

Opportunity

When Uke has his balance forward with his knees bent in a defensive posture: or when Uke escapes *Tsurikomi-ashi* or *De-ashi-barai* by jumping over Tori's attacking foot.

Timing

As Uke is about to place his weight on or take his weight off the leg to be attacked: or when Tori is able to draw Uke forward so that his balance is over the foot to be attacked.

The Throw

Tori breaks Uke's balance upwards and forward. If Uke has his knees bent, a powerful upward pull will be required to loosen his secure footing on the mat. Tori turns to his left on his right foot, to move out of Uke's line of movement, keeping his back and left leg—which is used for the throw—straight. His right leg should be bent slightly at the knee to lower his hips and assist his balance.

FIG 90

The throw is completed by Tori pivoting his hips in an anti-clockwise direction, bringing the sole of his left foot—with the leg absolutely straight—just below Uke's knee, and pulling Uke hard to his front and upwards with a powerful arm and body movement (Fig. 90).

Additional power can be generated by Tori driving his hips forward as he makes his turn.

Variations

If Tori is shorter than Uke

The lift will be upwards from underneath, with Tori possibly turning his wrists upwards for extra drive.

If Tori is taller than Uke

The lift will be a normal one from above.

Successive Attack with the Same Throw

This is not an easy technique to attempt successively since Uke is often firmly entrenched after the initial attack has failed. If he has been able to withstand the first attempt, a second try would have little chance of success. *Hiza-guruma* is itself generally used as a second attack after a different throw has failed.

Change of Throw in the Same Direction

If Uke is defensive when Tori attempts the throw, it is difficult for him to whip his leg out of the way of the throw. More often than not, Uke will move his right foot forward, bending it a little more and placing it securely on the mat (Fig. 91A). Tori may then turn to his left, replacing his left foot on the mat when it has passed behind and round his own right foot (Fig. 91B), and whipping his right hip and leg through (Fig. 91C) for *Harai-goshi*. In this instance *Harai-goshi* differs slightly from the way it is usually taught

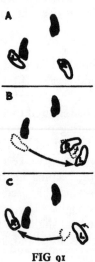

FIG 91

in that the sweep is made a little higher (Fig. 92). The object of this is to avoid sweeping painfully against Uke's knee in the event of it still being bent. In Figure 92 Uke has been straightened up by the power of Tori's pull—but the high sweep is made just the same. It's better to be safe than sorry.

FIG 92

Change of Direction of Attack

To prevent the throw, Uke may leave himself open to his rear. Which leg Tori should now attack depends upon the relative positions of the contestants and also upon which leg Uke has placed his weight. If his weight is distributed evenly, it does not matter which leg Tori attacks.

If Uke has thrown his weight on his right foot, Tori can break Uke's balance to his rear and bring his left leg through, between Uke's legs, to attack the right leg with *O-uchi-gari* to the left. Or he might use *O-soto-gari* against the right leg, reaping with his own right leg.

If Uke's weight is on his left foot, Tori can attack that leg also with *O-uchi-gari* or *O-soto-gari*.

Possible Counters to Hiza-guruma

These are the same as for *Tsurikomi-ashi* (page 58).

ASHI-GURUMA—LEG WHEEL

Opportunity

When Uke has his balance forward, or when Tori is able to bring it forward. It is a throw which is possible against an opponent adopting a defensive posture and is most suitable for a tall man.

63

Timing

As Uke is about to bring his weight upon the leg to be attacked. Or, should Tori be able to draw Uke forward, as Uke advances one leg.

The Throw

Tori breaks Uke's balance to his front, lifting at the same time. If Uke is holding out with his arms, Tori pulls Uke's arms outwards as he lifts.

Tori then turns to his left, taking his left hip and leg back. Stretching out his right leg, he places the hook at the Achilles tendon at the back of his right anklc *on* or *just below* Uke's right knee (Fig. 93). If the contact is made above the knee, Uke will be able to resist sufficiently to escape.

Tori continues to pull, punching his left hip back at the conclusion of the turn. Uke should be thrown over Tori's right leg to the mat.

FIG 93

Close bodily contact is not required. When in position for the throw, Tori's contact with Uke is only by way of his foot and he has insufficient leverage to make a sweep. Firm backward pressure is what is needed.

Variations

If Tori is shorter than Uke

Tori can drop under Uke's defensive arms and thrust up and to Uke's front with his own arms.

If Tori is taller than Uke

No variation to the throw is required. If he is substantially taller, however, he should be able to obtain a very powerful lift with his arms and develop a useful technique.

64

Successive Attack with the Same Throw

This is not a throw which lends itself to successive attack, although it may well open Uke up for a different throw.

Change of Throw in the Same Direction

As Uke checks the throw, Tori can lower his body and attack with *Tai-otoshi*. Or, if Tori is very supple, he might drive in under Uke's arms for *Seoi-nage*.

Should Uke defend by bracing himself against Tori's right leg (with the foot positions as shown in Fig. 94A), Tori, holding Uke off balance, could bring his right foot back to the mat behind his left foot (Fig. 94B) to attack Uke's right leg with *Tsurikomi-ashi* (Fig. 94C) or *Hiza-guruma*. This much lower attack is very often successful.

If Uke is crouching, *Hiza-guruma* or *Uchi-mata* may succeed.

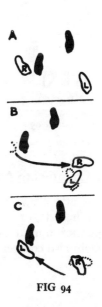

FIG 94

Change of Direction of Attack

This can be accomplished if Uke should throw his weight to his rear or, let us say, to his right. In such circumstances, Tori pivots to his right on his left foot (Fig. 95A), pinning Uke back on his heels by turning his wrists downwards and sliding his right leg round Uke's right leg (Fig. 95B) so that the hook just above the back of his heel is at the back of Uke's knee (Figs. 95C and 96). From this position, Tori makes a long-range *O-soto-gari* or, hopping in on his left foot, attacks with the normal form of the throw. *O-uchi-gari* is another possibility.

Alternatively, Uke's left leg could be attacked with *O-uchi-gari*.

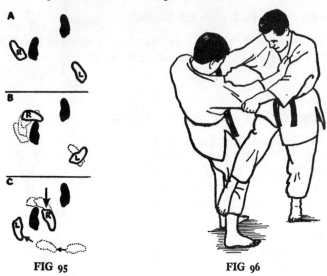

FIG 95   FIG 96

Possible Counters to Ashi-guruma

As he is attacked, Uke might brace his attacked right leg and, pivoting to his left, bring the sole of his left foot against the back of Tori's left knee to make a counter to his rear.

Uke might also counter with *Yoko-sutemi*.

TAI-OTOSHI—BODY DROP

Opportunity

When Uke is defending with stiff arms and legs fairly straight, or when he is brought into this stance by Tori's attack.

Timing

Whenever Uke's balance can be brought forward, particularly over his right foot.

66

The Throw

Tori breaks Uke's balance forward and upwards, pulling outwards at the same time to separate Uke's arms, and turns to his left on his right foot—taking his left hip and leg back in as long an arc as possible. He must keep his weight and balance well over his left hip and foot, bending the left knee as much as he can (Fig. 97). At the throwing point, he must have his left foot turned well to the left.

FIG 97

To conclude the throw, Tori maintains his forward pull and thrusts his right leg out so that the hook at the back of his heel presses firmly against the front of Uke's right shin. At the same time, he drives his left hip round and back—still in the same circle. The combined drive of hips and arms produces a very powerful throw.

Tori must have his balance well forward for this throw, as another glance at Figure 97 will show. If

FIG 98

unable to reach Uke's right leg with his own right leg, however, it will avail him nothing to merely try to reach back from the same stance. What he must do is bend his left knee even more, which will permit him to stretch back further with his right leg (Fig. 98).

Variations

If Tori is shorter than Uke

Tori should drop under Uke's defensive arms, driving them upwards as he does so, to make the throw at closer range. The fact that this will make his body more compact means that he will generate greater power.

If Tori is taller than Uke

Tori will apply his upward lift from above, weakening Uke's defence by pulling his arms outwards at the same time. He will also have the advantage of being able to make contact with Uke's right foot at long range.

Successive Attack with the Same Throw

If Uke has escaped the throw by stepping over Tori's right leg, Tori should hold Uke off balance to his front, maintaining the lift and drive to Uke's front, and step round a little further with his left foot. He can do this by pressing the toes of his right foot on the mat for a second and gliding his left foot about twelve inches along the mat. He will then be able to glide his right leg out again in front of Uke's and repeat his throw.

Where Uke has blocked the throw by bending and bracing his right leg against Tori's right

FIG 99

FIG 100

leg (Fig. 99), the method described above could equally well be employed. Alternatively, Tori can lean to his own front, in the direction in which the toes of his left foot point, by bending his left knee and ankle. At the same time, he must bend his right knee so that it is almost on the mat (Fig. 100). This will bring his right leg well below Uke's knee—thus defeating Uke's defence. Tori now straightens his right leg and attempts the throw again.

Change of Throw in the Same Direction

The throw used will depend upon the comparative heights of the contestants. If Uke is the taller, Tori might use *Seoi-nage*; but if Tori is the taller, he could attempt *Harai-goshi*. As a combination throw, *Seoi-nage* is often made with the right leg back (Fig. 101), rather like *Seoi-otoshi*.

Another possibility where Tori is the taller is for him to continue his turn, bringing his right arm round and over Uke's right arm to attempt *Maki-komi* (Fig. 102).

No matter which successive attack is used after Uke has succeeded in stepping over Tori's outstretched right leg, Tori will have to move his leg and replace it on the mat once more outside Uke's right leg, as in the original attempt.

If Uke's step-over has been a long one, Tori might attempt *Harai-goshi*. And side Sacrifice throws, such as *Yoko-wakare*, would also be effective.

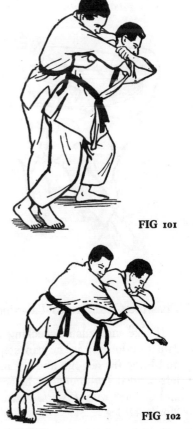

FIG 101

FIG 102

Change of Direction of Attack

Since the throw is usually made at long range, it is not easy to change direction. An opportunity arises, however, if Uke braces himself against Tori's right leg, throwing his balance backwards. Tori should slide his right foot round behind Uke's right ankle, holding Uke down with his left hand to prevent him stepping backwards and pushing to Uke's right back corner with the right arm (Fig. 103).

An alternative, using somewhat similar methods, is for Tori to slide his right leg between Uke's legs and round Uke's left leg from the inside. Tori then grips Uke's right trouser-leg near the end and pulls to Uke's front, at the same time driving to Uke's rear with his shoulder and body (Fig. 104).

FIG 103   FIG 104

Possible Counters to Tai-otoshi

If Uke succeeds in checking the throw as soon as Tori has moved into position for it, he can step over Tori's outstretched right foot and bring his left hip and leg in front of his opponent to attack with left-handed *Tai-otoshi*; or he could pivot to the left on his right foot and counter with *Ko-uchi-gari* on Tori's right leg or a rear throw on Tori's left leg.

OKURI-ASHI-HARAI—SWEEPING ANKLE THROW

Opportunity

When Uke makes a sideways move to his left.

Timing

As Uke, having moved his left foot, brings his right foot into the new position. Tori must attack before Uke can replace his right foot on the mat.

The Throw

Uke steps sideways to his left with his left foot and commences to move his right foot to regain his original stance. Tori steps to his right with his right foot, turning it a little to his right and closely following Uke's movement. As Uke moves his right foot, Tori sweeps along the mat with his left foot, turning it so that the sole makes contact with the outside of Uke's right ankle. Tori's left leg, hip and side should be kept in a straight line throughout. As he sweeps, Tori's left arm drives to his right and upwards while his right arm drives to his left and upwards (Fig. 105), the effect being that of turning a huge wheel. During this operation, Tori's right leg will be bent slightly at the knee to give him balance.

This throw might also be made against an opponent who is stepping forward, the timing being just as his right foot passes his left foot.

FIG 105

Variations

If Tori is shorter than Uke

Tori can drive with his arms under Uke's arms, developing a particularly powerful drive with his left because of the compactness of his body.

If Tori is taller than Uke

Tori can obtain substantial lift from above by spreading his elbows as he lifts. Momentum will derive from the lean of his body to his left and the drive of his hips to his right as the throw is made.

Successive Attack with the Same Throw

An opportunity for a second attempt is extremely unlikely to present itself.

Change of Throw in the Same Direction

In avoiding the throw, Uke may take his right foot back—in which case, Tori could attempt *Tsurikomi-ashi* or *Hiza-guruma* with his left foot against Uke's withdrawn right leg. *Tomoe-nage* or *Yoko-wakare* might equally well succeed.

If Tori is able to pivot to his left, other possibilities are *Harai-goshi* and *Tai-otoshi*.

Change of Direction of Attack

If Uke should throw his weight back, left-handed *O-soto-gari* might be attempted. Otherwise, this throw does not lend itself to change of direction.

Possible Counters to Okuri-ashi-harai

Uke could withdraw the leg being attacked and follow up Tori's attacking leg to apply *Okuri-ashi-harai* in return.

Alternatively, Uke could withdraw his right foot at the moment of attack and immediately replace it on the mat to pivot into *Tai-otoshi* or *O-soto-gari*.

All of the throws so far described are to Uke's front. Now follow the leg techniques to Uke's rear—more difficult to bring off in contest because it is harder to prevent Uke from escaping to his rear.

O-SOTO-GARI—MAJOR OUTER REAPING

Opportunity

When Uke has his balance inclined to his rear; or when, while in a static position, he bends his knees.

Timing

When Uke has his right leg firmly planted on the mat, or when Tori is able to pin it down.

The Throw

Tori steps in and pulls Uke to the front, a little upwards and outwards. It is important that Tori does not bend forward. He must keep his back straight. And his outward pull needs to be particularly strong against Uke's right arm in order to take it out of the line of attack (Fig. 106). This movement brings the right side of Tori's chest against that of Uke (Fig. 107). To complete the throw, Tori reaps Uke's right leg away with his own right leg, driving it back along the line of the mat. At the same time, he brings his body forward to force Uke backwards and down. For the final stage of the throw, Tori's body is stretched forward with his trunk and leg in a straight line, almost parallel with the mat (Fig. 108).

FIG 106

FIG 107

An alternative method of achieving the same end is for Tori to move in with his left foot, taking Uke's right arm down with his left hand and pressing down with his right hand against Uke's left shoulder—thus pinning Uke down upon his right heel (Fig. 109). The throw is completed by Tori reaping Uke's right leg and driving Uke downwards with his arms. This final drive must not be directly backwards but down to a point behind Uke's heels.

FIG 108   FIG 109

Variations

If Tori is shorter than Uke
Tori must drive Uke's defensive arm sideways to get close in for the throw.

If Tori is taller than Uke
He can afford to make the throw without being too close to Uke.

Successive Attack with the Same Throw

Should the throw "stick"—that is, should Uke manage to check the throw without disturbing Tori's balance and opening him up for a counter—Tori can often succeed by continuing his reap, but pivoting to his left as he does so. This completely changes the direction of the throw and catches Uke resisting in the wrong direction. Other than this, a successive attack is difficult.

If Tori fails to step in far enough with his left foot for the original attempt, he may be able to hop forward a few inches on his left foot and try again.

Change of Throw in the Same Direction

Once fully committed to *O-soto-gari*, it is not easy to change the throw. However, should Uke brace himself on his left foot, Tori could change to *O-soto-guruma* by bending his left knee even more and stretching out his right leg to his right, trapping Uke's left leg as well as his right (Fig. 110). A change to *O-uchi-gari* might also succeed.

FIG 110

Change of Direction of Attack

Uke's natural reaction is to defend himself by throwing his weight and balance forward. Taking advantage of this, Tori can pivot to his left on his left foot and use his right hip and leg to reap Uke's legs from the mat in a form of *Harai-goshi* to Uke's right side (Fig. 111). Since Uke may have his right leg well bent or stretched forward, Tori might have to sweep rather higher than usual—above Uke's right knee and a little upwards—bringing his head and trunk down to keep his body and sweeping leg in a straight line.

FIG 111

Alternatively, as Uke leans forward or throws his balance forward, Tori can pull to his front and, withdrawing his right leg from behind Uke's leg, bend his left knee and pivot to his left on his left foot. Then, keeping his body straight and continuing the turn to his left, he should fall to the mat on his left side, at Uke's front, in a form of *Yoko-wakare* (Fig. 112). If successful, Uke should be hurled over Tori's body, to take a very heavy fall.

Tomoe-nage might also be used successfully.

FIG 112

Possible Counters to O-soto-gari

There are three suggestions here. The first is for Uke to resist by thrusting his hips forward and then countering with an *O-soto-gari* of his own.

Secondly, if Tori is attacking his right leg, Uke can resist by thrusting his hips forward and turning a little to his right to counter with *Sukui-nage* or *Ushiro-goshi*.

For *Sukui-nage*, Uke may have to bring his right hand to Tori's belt or trouser leg; then, by thrusting his hips forward and lifting with his right hand, he will be able to scoop Tori up and throw him to his back.

For *Ushiro-goshi*, Uke will have to throw his arms round Tori's waist from the rear and, thrusting his hips forward, lift Tori from the mat. A turn to the left as Tori is lifted will allow Uke to bring his opponent to the mat.

The third possibility is for Uke to take a short step to his left as Tori makes his reap with his right foot, lifting his right foot so that Tori's reap sweeps past. At this point, Uke turns to his right, taking Tori round in that direction with his arms, and counters with a left-handed hand throw.

KO-UCHI-GARI—MINOR INNER REAPING

Opportunity

When Uke has his legs a little too widely spread; or, when in a defensive posture, he has his weight and balance inclined to his rear—either event resulting in a lack of mobility.

Timing

When Uke has his balance upon the foot to be attacked; or when his balance is equally distributed.

The Throw

Tori brings his left foot round in a clockwise circle, the sole making contact with the back of Uke's left foot at the Achilles tendon and drawing Uke's foot forward in the direction in which Uke's toes are pointing. To prevent Uke from escaping with a backward step, Tori should pull him forward and a little upward at the commencement of the attack, continuing the wrist and arm movement in a circle to thrust Uke down over his own heels (Fig. 113)—particularly to the rear of his left heel—as he draws Uke's foot forward.

In a powerful alternative movement, Tori attacks in exactly the

FIG 113

FIG 114

same way but, at the climax of the throw, uses his arms as if he were drawing a bow left-handed. That is to say, he pulls in with his left arm, to prevent Uke from stepping back, and thrusts forward directly over Uke's left heel with his right arm. In doing this, he turns his right wrist down, driving Uke back and downwards with a powerful body action (Fig. 114).

Variations

If Tori is shorter than Uke
He will have to attack at close range, using his body to drive Uke back.

If Tori is taller than Uke
The throw can be made from fairly long range, with Tori using his superior height to bear directly down on his opponent in the final drive.

Successive Attack with the Same Throw

This throw does not lend itself to successive attack because Uke, in his defence, will either step too far back to make a second attempt feasible or plant himself so firmly on the mat that Tori will be unable to reap his foot.

If Uke should step back only a short distance on his right foot, however, Tori can step or hop in on his right foot and continue to reap Uke's left foot, pivoting to his right as he does so.

Should Uke escape the first attempt by taking his left foot back over Tori's attacking foot, Tori may be able to change his attack to Uke's right foot with his own right foot.

Change of Throw in the Same Direction

If Uke escapes by taking his attacked left leg back, leaving his right leg well forward, Tori can come in for a left *O-uchi-gari.*

If Uke succeeds in freeing his left leg from the pull of Tori's left foot but replaces it on the mat in the same position, Tori can reach in with his right foot and attack with *O-soto-gari.* Should he be unable to get in sufficiently for a correct *O-soto-gari,* Tori can pivot to his left a little and make a throw to Uke's right rear which is partly *O-soto-gari* and partly a form of *Harai-goshi* (Fig. 115).

O-soto-gari to the left is also possible.

Change of Direction of Attack

Should Uke free his attacked foot and take it back so that his right foot leads, he opens himself for *Harai-goshi, Uchi-mata, Tai-otoshi* or *Ashi-guruma*. The choice of throw must depend on the relative positions of the contestants. If Uke's arms are stiff, *Tai-otoshi* or *Ashi-guruma* would most likely succeed; but if he crouches and bends his knees, then *Uchi-mata* might be a wiser choice.

FIG 115

Possible Counters to Ko-uchi-gari

Uke frees the attacked foot, steps over Tori's left foot with it and immediately replaces it on the mat. From this position, he can counter with *O-soto-gari* against Tori's right leg, *Hiza-guruma* or *O-uchi-gari* against his left leg or, by pivoting to his right, with left *Tai-otoshi*.

O-UCHI-GARI—MAJOR INNER REAPING

Opportunity

When Uke adopts a defensive posture with knees bent and legs fairly wide apart—particularly if his balance is inclined to his rear.

Timing

When Uke's feet, or at least the foot to be attacked, may be pinned to the mat.

The Throw

Tori moves Uke slightly forward and upwards with his arms and wrists, moving his own left foot forward. The movement with his arms is circular—first forward, to Uke's front, and upwards; and then over to Uke's rear. Coincident with this, Tori brings his right leg between Uke's legs to reap Uke's left leg away to his front. Thrusting forward with his body, Tori drives Uke downwards to the rear of the leg being reaped (Fig. 116).

If Tori is able, in his initial attack, to get in close enough for his chest to make contact with Uke's, he will have the extra power and weight of his body to drive Uke down. There is the danger, though, that Tori might also fall. In such an event, he would have to avoid falling on Uke by making a forward roll on his right arm over Uke's left shoulder.

FIG 116

Variations

If Tori is shorter than Uke
He will have to move in close to Uke, driving in under Uke's defensive arms. Emphasis will be on the lift and reap.

If Tori is taller than Uke
He will find it difficult to break through Uke's defensive arms and will have to make the throw from long range, using his height to lift and then drive Uke to the mat. Emphasis will be on the final drive to the mat.

Successive Attack with the Same Throw

Uke is almost certain to defend by holding Tori away, thus throwing his arm-balance forward. He will not, therefore, be in a posture which makes a second attempt possible.

Change of Throw in the Same Direction

Here, again, Uke's defensive posture will give scant opportunity for any throw in the same direction . . . unless he throws his balance over one leg, in which case *O-soto-gari* becomes a possibility.

Change of Direction of Attack

O-uchi-gari is valuable in that it opens up a defensive judoman for an attacker who is sufficiently fast and well-balanced to change his direction of throw from Uke's rear to his front.

If Uke takes his right leg back, Tori can pivot to his left to attack with *Tai-otoshi*. And if he can get in close enough to Uke, *Harai-goshi* is possible.

Figure 117A shows how, by taking his right leg back, Uke provides an opening to his right front; and Figure 117B shows the opening to his left front if he takes his left leg back.

There might also be an opening for *Tomoe-nage*.

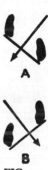

FIG 117

Possible Counters to O-uchi-gari

By withdrawing his attacked leg over Tori's attacking leg, Uke will be in a position to counter with *Uki-goshi*, *O-uchi-gari*, *O-soto-gari*, *Ko-uchi-gari* or left-handed *O-soto-gari*, the choice dictated by the relative positions of the contestants resulting from the defensive action.

Alternatively, as Tori attacks with his right leg, Uke can move in with his left hip to make contact with Tori's right hip and block the throw. He can then counter as above-mentioned.

KO-SOTO-GARI—MINOR OUTER REAPING

Opportunity

When Uke and Tori are fairly close together—Uke having the foot to be attacked advanced, or at least within reach of Tori.

Timing

When Uke is about to place his weight upon the foot to be attacked. Or when, with his weight upon it or having turned a little sideways to Tori, he brings the foot to be attacked close to Tori's attacking foot.

The Throw

If the contestants are facing each other, Tori steps to his left and forward with his right foot, turning it to his right as he does so. At the same time, by using his wrists, he pins Uke down on his right heel. (If at first Tori pulls Uke in and upwards, he may be able to induce a backward-pulling reaction from Uke which Tori can follow up with the downward pressure, using his wrists in a circular movement.) Tori then brings the sole of his left foot behind Uke's right heel (Fig. 118) and draws it in the direction in which Uke's toes are pointing, pressing Uke to the rear of his right heel with arms and body (Fig. 119).

FIG 118

FIG 119

Should Uke be rather a long way from Tori at the commencement of the attack, Tori might step round Uke's right side with the left foot (Fig. 120A), bring up the right (Fig. 120B) and then sweep with the left (Fig. 120C)—three separate movements.

If Uke turns himself sideways to Tori—perhaps in an attempt to avoid a throw—Tori can attack with practically no initial foot movement, for Uke will have placed himself in the position for which Tori usually has to manoeuvre.

Even when Uke's foot is firmly on the mat, the throw can be made by drawing it very determinedly forward and driving Uke backwards to the rear of his own heels.

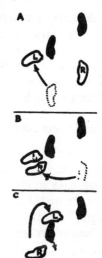

FIG 120

Variations

If Tori is shorter than Uke

The throw must be made at close range, with Tori lifting and stepping under Uke's arms. Then, by changing the direction of the thrust, Tori drives Uke down to the rear of his own right heel. As Tori draws Uke's right foot forward he pins Uke down with his left hand, straightening his left arm with the fist pointing downwards—as if he were attempting to punch at a spot on the mat just to the rear of Uke's right heel. His right arm, driving against Uke's collar bone or chest, presses Uke down in the same direction.

If Tori is taller than Uke

The throw is made at longer range, with Tori making use of his height and reach to stretch Uke out backwards on the mat—tending to drive to Uke's rear rather than downwards.

Successive Attack with the Same Throw

Uke's defensive tactics may leave him open to a second attempt, in which case Tori continues the downward and rear drive with his arms, stepping in more on his right foot to place it at the side of Uke's right foot and reap again. It may be necessary to change the direction of this attack slightly to overcome the defence.

Change of Throw in the Same Direction

Placing his left foot back on the mat, Tori can attack with *O-soto-gari*.

An alternative is a form of *Yoko-wakare*. Keeping Uke pinned down over his own right heel, Tori bends his right knee—as if sitting on his heel—and, keeping his left leg straight, glides his left foot along the mat so that his leg is stretched out behind and close to Uke's right heel. As he does this, Tori turns or rolls to his left, throwing Uke backwards over his left leg.

Change of Direction of Attack

A throw to the right is not easy since Tori has moved towards Uke's right side (Fig. 121A). To overcome this, Tori brings his left hip and leg back in a circular movement to his left before replacing his foot on the mat (Fig. 121D). He then attacks, by bringing his right leg through (Fig. 121C), with *Harai-goshi* or *Tai-otoshi*.

A left-handed technique might be possible if Tori, already poised on his right foot, pivots on it to his right and brings his left leg and hip through between himself and Uke to attack with *Harai-goshi* or *Tai-otoshi*.

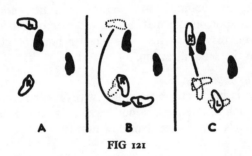

FIG 121

Possible Counters to Ko-soto-gari

If Uke is able to block Tori's throw by bracing his attacked foot on the mat, he can counter with *Tai-otoshi* or *O-uchi-gari* against Tori's right leg.

If he escapes by stepping back over Tori's attacking left foot, Uke will be in position to counter with *O-soto-gari* or *Ko-soto-gari*.

CHAPTER VI

Koshi-Waza – Hip Techniques

The *Koshi-Waza* group is a large one which includes many of the most popular judo throws, such as *O-goshi* and *Harai-goshi*—which are almost always taught to beginners although they are not easy.

In all hip techniques, Tori has to sink low by bending his knees; and in some, like *O-goshi* and *Tsurikomi-goshi*, he must sink very low indeed. Despite this, it is essential that he keeps his back straight and trunk upright. If he bends forward he will slump his weight on to his abdomen, congesting that area and losing the freedom to move his hips.

Tori should always turn the foot he finally stands on—the left, in right-handed throws—well round to his left, permitting himself a big turn when throwing and helping to maintain his balance.

FIG 122

It may be that at the conclusion of Tori's turn Uke still maintains contact with the mat (Fig. 122). Even if only slight, that contact provides a chance of escape and counter. But Tori, if he has turned his left foot sufficiently to his left, can overcome it by leaning to his left front corner. This will take Uke's feet off the mat without any physical effort on the part of Tori (Fig. 123) and allow the throw to be completed.

85

If Tori's weight is equally placed between his feet when he is in the position shown in Figure 122, Uke might ride round his right hip and escape. To prevent this, Tori should transfer his balance to his left foot and thus leave Uke balanced helplessly on his right hip. Additionally, Tori's right leg will now be free should he wish to change the throw from, say, *O-goshi* to *Harai-goshi*.

When performing *Koshi-waza*, Tori must apply lift to Uke throughout. He commences by pulling Uke forward and upwards, and this lift must be maintained until *ippon*. It is a point that needs watching, because it is only too easy for Tori to change his upward lift to a downward pull half way through the throw without realising he is doing so.

FIG 123

O-GOSHI—MAJOR HIP THROW

Opportunity

When, in close contact, Tori is able to sink his hips below Uke's.

Timing

When, with Uke fairly upright, Tori is able to move in close: or, having attacked unsuccessfully with a throw such as *Harai-goshi*, can slide his arm round Uke's body.

The Throw

Tori attacks with an upward and forward pull, having manoeuvred or stepped in close. To step in, which takes an extra movement, he turns to his left (Fig. 124A), taking his left foot back so that it passes close behind his right heel and replacing it on the mat a little further back than his right foot and about twelve inches from it (Fig. 124B). At about the half way point of the turn, Tori releases the grip of his right hand and drops his arm to his side (Fig. 125) in a relaxed manner. He then moves the arm round Uke's body as the turn continues. This must be done without conscious effort. If he signals his intention, Uke will react with a check to the movement. As Tori's arm comes round Uke's body, Tori pulls Uke to his front and applies lift upwards. Tori should attempt to turn more than 180° so that his left hip drives into Uke and forces him over his right hip. To complete the throw, Tori transfers all his weight and balance to his left foot and leans a little to his left front corner (Fig. 126).

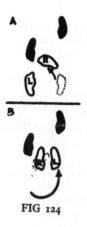

FIG 124

FIG 125

FIG 126

Variations

If Tori is shorter than Uke

He will have the natural advantage of his hips being lower than Uke's and will be able to attack under Uke's defensive arms. If he is considerably shorter than Uke, however, he will find it difficult to complete the throw and might find *Tsurikomi-goshi* or a shoulder technique more effective.

If Tori is taller than Uke

He will have to sink very low and use considerable pull to straighten Uke's body. If he is very much taller than Uke, it would be better for him not to use this throw.

Successive Attack with the Same Throw

The throw is frequently avoided by Uke riding round Tori's right hip. In this case, Tori can pivot a little to his left—possibly taking his left foot back a few inches—and attempt the throw again.

If the first attempt is avoided by Uke stepping back with his right foot and pushing his hips forward, or by bending his knees and leaning back, Tori must maintain his lift on Uke with both arms and, at the same time, bend his knees to sink under Uke's defence (Fig. 127). Tori's right arm, which is round Uke's body, must at the same time lift upwards and drive Uke to his front.

FIG 127

Change of Throw in the Same Direction

Should Uke ride round Tori's right hip in his bid to escape, Tori can continue his attack with *Harai-goshi* or *Tai-otoshi*—but he must maintain his pull to Uke's front as he changes his throw.

Koshi-Waza—Hip Techniques

Change of Direction of Attack

Instead of escaping round Tori's
hip, Uke might well defend himself by taking his right leg and hip
back and perhaps throwing his
right shoulder back in order to
break Tori's left-hand grip on his
jacket. This makes a forward
throw virtually impossible: so
Tori pivots to his right on his left
foot and breaks Uke's balance
to his left rear, bringing his right
leg between Uke's legs to attack
with *O-uchi-gari* against Uke's
left leg. As he turns, Tori may
recover his left-hand hold on
Uke's jacket. But if instead he
maintains his hold round Uke's

FIG 128

body, he must avoid having his hand under Uke's body as the throw is
completed.

If Uke has defended by bending his knees and leaning back, Tori
can pivot to his right a little and slide his right heel round behind
Uke's right knee. By breaking Uke's balance to his rear and pulling
Uke's leg to his front, a long-range *O-soto-gari* can be made (Fig. 128).

Possible Counters to O-goshi

The leg on which Tori stands as he turns in for the throw could
be swept away by means of an ankle technique. Or Uke could bring
his left foot up behind Tori's left knee and throw him to his rear. Tori
could also be countered with a side Sacrifice technique.

A powerful counter can be made by checking Tori's turn and
moving in for a left-handed *O-goshi* or left-handed *Tai-otoshi*.

Utsuru-goshi is the classic counter—but very difficult.

UKI-GOSHI—FLOATING HIP THROW

Opportunity

As for *O-goshi*, with Uke in a more defensive posture.

89

Timing

When Uke is fairly upright or in a position which allows Tori to attack very low under his arms.

The Throw

Tori pulls Uke firmly upwards to his front, applying powerful outward pull if Uke is holding out. As he does this, he turns to his left—stepping in, if necessary—and drives his right hip, in a circular movement, back into Uke's body and upwards. Tori's right hip makes contact just under Uke's right hip (Fig. 129). As he continues to turn, Tori maintains his upward and forward pull with his left arm; but his right arm, quite relaxed, slides round Uke's body, where it adds to the upward and forward pull. By going on with his turn, Tori floats Uke upwards and then off his hip to the mat.

FIG 129

Tori may have to take two short steps to position himself as he break's Uke's balance with his arms—perhaps because Uke is holding him out with fairly stiff arms and leaning forward to make a gap between them. He would still pull Uke forward and upwards, but this time also applying outward pull to separate Uke's arms (Fig. 130) and stepping in with his right foot, turning it to his left (Fig. 131A). Immediately his right foot is on the mat, Tori

FIG 130

90

must pivot on it and bring his left foot into position very quickly so that his stance is a little more than sideways on to Uke (Fig. 131B).

Variations

If Tori is shorter than Uke

Tori attacks under Uke's arms, driving them upwards from below. If Tori is much shorter than Uke, however, this would not be a good choice of throw.

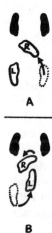

A

If Tori is taller than Uke

Lifting upwards and forwards, Tori's height will be an advantage in pulling Uke on to his hip. This technique is, in fact, eminently suited to a tall judoman.

B   FIG 13

Successive Attack with the Same Throw

Should Uke defend by stiffening his arms only, Tori might be able to attack again, using powerful upward and outward pull. And if Uke escapes by bending his knees, it is possible that Tori could lift sufficiently to make a second attack. But by and large, this is not a throw for successive attack.

Change of Throw in the Same Direction

The advantage of *Uki-goshi* is that it can be changed without a lot of extra movement. If Uke defends by bending his knees, Tori could use *Harai-goshi* or *Tai-otoshi*; if he moves round Tori's right hip, *Harai-goshi* or *Ashi-guruma* could well succeed. Uke might double up a little at the waist in an escape round Tori's hip, in which case Tori should sweep upwards with his *Harai-goshi*.

Change of Direction of Attack

If Uke resists by bending his knees and leaning back, Tori should slide his right foot round behind Uke's right knee so that the "hook" at Tori's Achilles tendon presses behind Uke's knee. At the same time, Tori should change his pull to Uke's front to a thrust down to the rear of Uke's right heel, pulling his opponent's right leg forward (Fig. 132) and throwing him to the right rear corner.

If Uke defends by stepping back with his right leg, Tori can bring his right leg between Uke's legs and attack with *O-uchi-gari*.

FIG 132

Possible Counters to Uki-goshi

Because Tori only turns about 90°, this is not as easy as some other hip throws to counter. Uke could move his hips in to block Tori's turn and then attempt a hip throw or *Harai-goshi*. Or, once Tori has moved in for his throw, Uke could check it—perhaps by thrusting his hips forward—and counter with a rear Sacrifice throw.

HARAI-GOSHI—SWEEPING LOIN OR HIP THROW

Opportunity

When Uke is fairly upright. He may be bent forward at the waist: but he should not be attacked if he has his knees bent.

Timing

Whenever it is possible to break Uke's balance to his front.

The Throw

Tori breaks Uke's balance forward and upwards, pivoting to
the left on his right foot and
taking his left hip back and round
as far as he is able (Fig. 133A), his
object being to straighten Uke's
body and legs. Completing his
turn, Tori transfers his weight
and balance to his left foot,
thrusting back with his right hip
and leg (Fig. 133B) across the
front of Uke's legs (Fig. 134). The
throw is made by driving back the
hips—the right hip thrusting
back against Uke's legs. This
thrust, combined with the drive
of Tori's arms to Uke's front, will
bring Uke over to the mat.

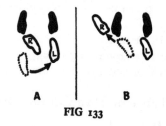

FIG 133

Tori's sweep must be low and
directly backwards, with very
little lift to his leg. Obviously,
the higher up Uke's legs the
sweep is made the more of Uke's
weight Tori will have to overcome.

FIG 134

If Tori is shorter than Uke

Tori can drive Uke's arms upwards as well as to his front, thus
attacking from beneath Uke's arms with a very powerful upward
thrust.

If Tori is taller than Uke

As Uke's arms are certain to be straightened in defence, Tori will
use his height to pull upward and outward as well as to his front.
By so doing, he will be able to move between Uke's arms to attack.

Successive Attack with the Same Throw

Since Tori should be fully committed to this throw, a second
attempt is not easy. However, if Uke defends by bending his knees

93

and crouching, Tori could increase his forward and upward pull and sweep again—this time applying some upward thrust from his right hip and leg.

In the event of Uke escaping by getting his right leg over or round Tori's sweeping right leg, Tori should pivot a little to his left on his left foot and sweep again.

Change of Throw in the Same Direction

If Uke defends by taking his right hip and leg back, perhaps throwing his weight to his left rear, Tori might be able to bend his left knee and stretch out his right leg to attack with *Tai-otoshi*. In doing so, Tori's right arm must be kept fairly straight, with just a slight curve to the left (Fig. 135), and he will pull in a wide circle to his left with his left arm.

Uke may escape the initial attempt by bringing his right leg over Tori's sweeping leg, leaving himself open for *Uchi-mata*—which Tori would effect by thrusting his right hip and leg back and turning to his left to make the throw.

FIG 135

Change of Direction of Attack

Once committed to *Harai-goshi*, it is impossible to change it from right to left: but opportunities to change to an attack to Uke's rear do occur.

Should Uke avoid the throw by throwing back his right hip, leg and shoulder, he places his balance on his left leg, giving Tori the chance to pivot to his right on his left foot and bring his right leg round Uke's left leg from the inside to attack with *O-uchi-gari*. As he does so, he breaks Uke's balance fast and hard to his left back corner, thrusting him down towards his left heel.

Uke might resist the initial attempt by bending his knees and leaning back. Again, *O-uchi-gari* would be effective. But an alternative would be for Tori to bring his right foot behind Uke's right knee to attack with *O-soto-gari.*

Possible Counters to Harai-goshi

If Tori is in close contact, Uke could attempt a rear hip throw or scooping throw: but if Tori succeeds in moving further into his throw, Uke should attempt a side Sacrifice counter such as *Yoko-sutemi* or *Yoko-wakare.*

TSURIKOMI-GOSHI—DRAWING HIP THROW

Opportunity

When Tori is able to turn and sink well below Uke's defence, with Uke's body upright or curved a little forward.

Timing

Whenever the opportunity presents itself.

The Throw

Tori pulls Uke forward and upwards—thrusting hard upwards and to Uke's front with his right arm. He bends his knees as he attacks

FIG 136   FIG 137

in order to get right under Uke's defence (Fig. 136). Maintaining the pull and upward thrust, Tori turns to his left on his right foot (Fig. 137), driving his left hip back into Uke (Fig. 138). In this position, Tori should have all his weight on his left foot although his right foot will be on the mat, leaning slightly to his left front corner—continuing to drive Uke upwards and forward over his right hip (Fig. 139).

Tori's right-arm thrust must be upwards and directly to Uke's front. The slightest deviation to the right will assist Uke to escape by moving round Tori's right hip.

Tsurikomi-goshi lends itself well to left-handed technique. The upward thrust with the left arm—the grip being on Uke's sleeve —enables Tori to get the throw under way without alerting Uke. And the grip on Uke's sleeve will provide greater leverage than one on his lapel.

FIG 138   FIG 139

Variations

If Tori is shorter than Uke

He has a natural advantage for getting underneath Uke's arms.

If Tori is taller than Uke

He must not attempt to gain his position by bending forward at the waist. If he is especially tall it would be better not to attempt this throw.

Successive Attack with the Same Throw

Once Tori has sunk low for his attempt, although he will be in a very good position to attack with a different throw, he will be insufficiently mobile to attempt the same throw again.

Change of Throw in the Same Direction

Uke will usually defend by throwing his weight back to his rear, or bending his knees so that Tori cannot get underneath him, or riding round Tori's hip. If he does the first mentioned, Tori might be able to take his left leg and hip back a little and then drive his hips back into Uke to throw him with *Seoi-nage*. Or he could attempt *Tai-otoshi* by thrusting out his right leg and driving Uke round and over it. *Tai-otoshi* might also be effective if Uke defends by bending his knees.

The best opportunity for a powerful forward throw comes, however, when Uke escapes round Tori's right hip. In this circumstance, Tori can thrust his right hip and leg back—the leg between Uke's legs—to perform *Uchi-mata*. Alternatively, he can thrust his right hip and leg across the front of Uke's right leg and sweep with *Harai-goshi*. Another possibility is for him to take his left hip and leg back and turn into *Seoi-nage*.

Another powerful throw can be made if Tori releases his right-hand hold on Uke's left lapel and brings his right arm over Uke's right arm, at the same time sliding his right leg across the front of Uke's right leg to turn to his left into *Maki-komi*.

Change of Direction of Attack

Should Uke defend by taking his right leg back and placing his weight on his left leg, Tori can pivot to his right on his left foot—so that he is almost facing Uke—and bring his right leg between Uke's legs to reap Uke's left leg with *O-uchi-gari* (Fig. 140).

If Uke defends by bending his knees and/or leaning back, Tori can pivot to his right on his left foot, bringing his right leg outside Uke's right leg and round it from behind. He can then use *O-soto-gari*, reaping Uke's leg and thrusting Uke to his rear and downwards. As Tori will have dropped very low for his initial *Tsurikomi-goshi*, he will be able to drive his right shoulder into Uke's body as he reaps, making a very powerful throw (Fig. 141).

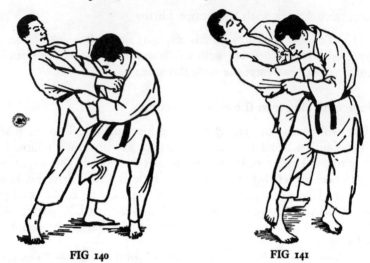

FIG 140   FIG 141

Possible Counters to Tsurikomi-goshi

If Uke blocks the throw by thrusting his left hip forward to meet Tori's right hip, he can counter with left-handed *O-goshi* or *Harai-goshi*. But if he throws his balance to his rear to avoid the attack, he can use *Yoko-sutemi* or a rear hand or hip throw.

HANE-GOSHI—SPRING HIP THROW

Opportunity

When Uke is fairly upright and his balance can be broken to his front.

Timing

Preferably when Uke's right leg is advanced.

The Throw

Tori manoeuvres Uke so that his right foot is fairly close to the toes of Uke's right foot, at the same time pulling Uke to his front and very firmly upwards. This straightens Uke's body and tilts it forward.

98

Continuing the pull, Tori turns to his left, pivoting on his right foot. His turn should not be as big as that for *O-goshi* or *Harai-goshi* but rather more like the one required for *Uki-goshi*, as the foot positions shown in Figure 142 indicate. As Tori completes his turn, he brings his right leg back against the front of Uke's shin with his foot to the inner side of Uke's right leg (Fig. 143). Without checking his movement, Tori leans forward, taking Uke with him, and thrusts Uke back—*not* upwards—with his right hip and leg, keeping his right side, hip and leg in a straight line and all in contact with Uke's body (Fig. 144). To complete the throw, Tori turns to his left on his left foot and throws or "springs" Uke off his leg to the mat.

FIG 142

FIG 143

Variations

If Tori is shorter than Uke

He will attack from underneath Uke's arms; but as contact is required at chest level, as well as at hip and leg level, he must pull in such a way as to separate Uke's arms. As he turns, his left hand will continue to pull to Uke's front and upwards. But by turning his right wrist upwards he can develop an upward thrust similar to that used in *Tsurikomi-goshi*.

FIG 144

99

If Tori is taller than Uke

He will use the advantage of his superior height to develop a really powerful upward lift. There is, however, the danger of the natural tendency to push Uke down instead of maintaining the upward lift throughout.

To obtain chest contact, Tori must drive in between Uke's arms, applying powerful outward pull as he attacks.

Successive Attack with the Same Throw

This is not the best of throws with which to attempt successive attack—although it is possible if Uke, keeping his legs fairly straight, holds out with straight arms. Tori would have to continue his forward, outward and upward pull from the position shown in Figure 145A and step in very fast, as indicated in Figure 145B, to attack again.

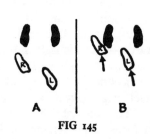

FIG 145

Change of Throw in the Same Direction

Provided Uke has remained reasonably upright after avoiding the throw, *Harai-goshi* could be successful. But if Uke escapes by crouching and bending his knees, Tori can step in with his left foot and attack with *Uchi-mata*.

Change of Direction of Attack

If Uke defends by leaning back—and especially if he bends his knees—Tori can slide his right foot round the back of Uke's right knee, turning on his left foot to his right as he does so in order to face Uke and throw him to his right back corner with a combination of long-range *O-soto-gari* and *Ashi-guruma*. Or, if Uke throws his weight on his left leg, Tori can attack with *O-uchi-gari* on Uke's left leg.

Possible Counters to Hane-goshi

These are the same as for *Uki-goshi* (page 92), *Harai-goshi* (page 95) or *Tsurikomi-goshi* (page 98).

MAKI-KOMI—WINDING THROW

Opportunity

When Uke is in a defensive posture, with knees bent and feet apart.

Timing

As Tori suceeds in bringing Uke's balance forward.

The Throw

This is a very violent throw which makes an effective follow-up to throws such as *Harai-goshi* or *Hane-goshi*.

Tori steps in with his right foot, or manoeuvres so that his right foot is fairly close to Uke's, without getting quite so close in as for *Harai-goshi*. He uses his arms to break Uke's balance, pulling direct to Uke's front and upwards, and turns to his left, pivoting on his right foot. Maintaining the pull with his left arm throughout, Tori releases his hold on Uke's jacket with his right hand at about half way through his turn and brings his right arm over Uke's right arm, being careful not to force downwards with it. He continues his turn, turning rather more than 180°, so that his left hip drives into Uke's body without checking the turn. This, combined with the pull on Uke's right arm, winds Uke over Tori's right hip to the mat (Fig. 146).

There is another form of this throw which is used by many contest men. It begins in exactly the same way, with Tori making his approach, pulling Uke to his front and upwards as he turns, and bringing his right arm over Uke's right arm to apply all the pull and lift on one side. But at this point, to prevent Uke stepping round Tori's right hip to escape, Tori stretches out his right foot so that the end of his calf or Achilles tendon presses

FIG 146

against the front or front right-
hand corner of Uke's right shin
(Fig. 147)—very like *Tai-otoshi*.
Then, keeping his right leg, hip
and side in a straight line, Tori
continues to turn until he drops
at Uke's right side, maintaining
full control but not falling *on* Uke
(Fig. 148).

FIG 147

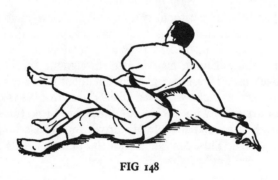

FIG 148

Variations

If Tori is shorter than Uke

In this circumstance the throw is a very difficult one, due to the
necessity of Tori bringing his right arm over Uke's, and Tori will
find the version shown in Figure 147 most suited to him. If the
difference in height is considerable, Tori will have to overcome
a strong tendency to pull down. Tori might decide that it would be
simpler to bring his right arm *under* Uke's right arm and thrust
upwards ... but this, of course, would make the throw *Seoi-otoshi*.

If Tori is taller than Uke

He will be able to bring his right arm over Uke's without a break
in his upward and forward lift.

Successive Attack with the Same Throw

With the basic form of the throw (Fig. 146), if Uke escapes by moving round Tori's right hip, Tori can move his left foot back and, in so doing, push out or project his right hip, placing himself in position to attack again with the same technique.

Alternatively, as Uke attempts to move round Tori's hip, Tori can thrust out his right leg and hip in front of Uke's right leg and so catch him with the form of the throw shown in Figure 147.

Change of Throw in the Same Direction

If Uke tries to escape round Tori's right hip, a form of *Harai-goshi* can be attempted. But if Uke resists by throwing his balance to his rear, Tori can continue to turn and wind, changing the throw to *Maki-harai-goshi* (Fig. 149). To accomplish this against Uke's backward balance, Tori must develop maximum power by leaning forward over his left leg to tilt Uke to his left front as much as possible.

FIG 149

Change of Direction of Attack

Change of direction can only be made to Uke's rear. So if Uke attempts to escape by throwing his weight and balance to his rear, Tori follows him—pivoting to his right on his left foot as he does so and bringing his right foot behind Uke's right knee. He now reaps with his right leg and drives his right shoulder into Uke's right chest, forcing him down to the mat, aiming at a point just behind Uke's heels (Fig. 150).

O-uchi-gari could be used in a similar manner.

FIG 150

Possible Counters to Maki-komi

Because it is such a powerful throw, *Maki-komi* is very difficult
to counter. The best thing for Uke to do is to step over Tori's outstretched right foot and attack with a rear throw.

The throw could be blocked by Uke sliding his left foot between
Tori's legs and placing his left foot against the front of Tori's left
shin, thus "wedging" himself into position.

UCHI-MATA—INNER THIGH THROW

Opportunity

When Uke adopts a defensive posture by bending his knees and
spreading his legs.

Timing

When Tori can manoeuvre close enough to Uke to draw him
upwards and forward.

The Throw

Tori places himself close to Uke, turning on his left foot—which he
has placed between Uke's feet with his heel just inside and in line with
Uke's left big toe. He may manoeuvre into this position so that all he
has to do is pivot on his left foot; persuade Uke to bring his right foot
well forward; or step in with his right foot (Fig. 151A), bring his left
foot round (Fig. 151B) and thrust his right foot back between Uke's
legs (Fig. 151C).

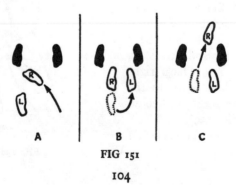

A   **B**   **C**

FIG 151

Another and much faster method is to jump in from the original stance (Fig. 152A) with the left foot when Uke has his right leg back (Fig. 152B), turning it to his left as he does so and then pivoting on it to his left to make the throw (Fig. 152C).

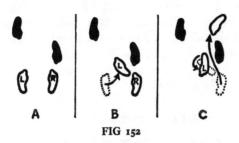

A   **B**   **C**

FIG 152

Tori is likely to have to over-come stiff arms as well as a defensive crouch, so he must break Uke's balance to his front and powerfully upwards as well as using outward pull to separate Uke's arms. And in order to drive underneath Uke's defence and get his right hip deeply in between Uke's legs, he must bend his left knee (Fig. 153). This thrust of right thigh and leg between Uke's legs is made as Tori turns to his left on his left foot. It is a thrust back—not up—and it sweeps Uke's legs from the mat. Tori's continued turn turns Uke over and throws him to the mat (Fig. 154).

FIG 153

FIG 154

Variations

If Tori is shorter than Uke
If the difference in height is not too great, Tori can come in as

described, driving under Uke to make the throw. But if Tori is much shorter than Uke, he may find the throw unsuitable—unless Uke has adopted a very deep crouch.

If Tori is taller than Uke

He will have the disadvantage of having to sink that much lower to get his hip between Uke's legs, and he will have to move between Uke's arms as he will be unable to attack underneath them. On the credit side, however, his height will help him to obtain considerable lift from above; and he will find it easier to separate Uke's arms by pulling outwards from above.

Successive Attack with the Same Throw

There is seldom an opportunity of making a second attempt with *Uchi-mata*. But should the throw fail because Tori has not managed to get sufficiently under Uke, Tori might be able to strengthen the pull with his arms, move his left leg back a little and attack again.

Change of Throw in the Same Direction

The usual defence against *Uchi-mata* is to throw the weight back and to the left or to push Tori away with the arms to prevent him getting his right hip into position. Should Uke throw his weight back, he can still be successfully attacked low down to his right side with throws such as *Tai-otoshi* and *Harai-goshi*—provided always that Tori has applied and maintained his pull to Uke's front.

Change of Direction of Attack

If Uke resists to his rear, Tori could pivot back to his right on his left foot and bring his right leg between Uke's leg to attack Uke's left leg with *O-uchi-gari*.

Possible Counters to Uchi-mata

Not easy to bring off, counters are usually to the attacker's rear and include *Suki-nage* (scooping throw), *Yoko-guruma* (side wheel), *Ushiro-goshi* (rear hip throw) and *Utsuri-goshi* (changing hip throw).

CHAPTER VII

Te-Waza – Shoulder, Arm and Hand Techniques

Shoulder throws are very popular, being not only effective but also graceful and spectacular. They require continuous control over the opponent, for even the slightest weakness will provide an opening for a counter.

All shoulder throws require close contact, with Tori moving between or beneath Uke's arms—but ever careful to avoid moving directly into them as they are straightened in defence.

IPPON-SEOI-NAGE—SHOULDER THROW ON ONE SIDE

Opportunity

When Uke is upright or leaning forward slightly.

Timing

When Tori is able to bring Uke close to him, either by manoeuvre or by moving himself.

The Throw

Tori places the toes of his right foot close to the toes of Uke's right foot, turning his foot to the left and bending his knee as he does so. At the same time, he draws Uke forward and upwards, also pulling a little outwards to separate his arms. He turns to his left, pivoting on his right foot.

When his turn has reached about 45°, Tori releases his hold on Uke's jacket with his right hand and brings that arm between his own body and Uke's and under Uke's right arm, where it at once assists the pull of Tori's left arm to Uke's front and upwards. Tori can grip Uke's jacket with his right hand at about the top of Uke's right shoulder (Fig. 155). From the position shown in Figure 155, Tori continues to turn, taking his left hip back and pulling Uke's right arm forward and upward. The upward pull is very important indeed, for the object is to draw Uke up over the right hip and finally over the shoulder to the mat (Fig. 156).

FIG 155

FIG 156

My own opinion is that the grip on Uke's jacket with the right hand automatically tends to pull Uke down towards the mat, spoiling the throw. Tori must continue to push upwards with his right arm. I prefer an alternative in which Tori continues to drive his right arm upwards so that it carries on the curve of his right side (Figs. 157 and 158). This drive takes Uke upwards in a most powerful way: and then, as Tori maintains his turn by taking his left hip back, his thrusting right arm continues the movement (Fig. 159).

FIG 157

FIG 158   FIG 159

Variations

If Tori is shorter than Uke

The throw can be performed in the orthodox way.

If Tori is taller than Uke

He will find the throw very difficult to perform, because he will have to come in very low. It would be advisable for him to use *Seoi-otoshi* instead.

Successive Attack with the Same Throw

The usual cause of failure here is that Tori has left a gap between himself and Uke (Fig. 160), and successive attack must be aimed at correcting the fault. Therefore, to attack again, Tori thrusts Uke upwards and to his front with his arms, bending his knees at the same time. He then takes a series of short, rapid steps back, driving his hips back into Uke (Fig. 161). When contact is achieved, the continued backward drive of Tori's hips and the forward and upward thrust of his arms will drive Uke to the mat.

Change of Throw in the Same Direction

If Uke avoids the throw by moving round Tori's right side and hip as Tori turns, Tori can effect a throw by changing to *Harai-goshi*, *Tai-otoshi* or *Maki-komi*.

FIG 160   FIG 161

If Uke escapes by throwing his weight and balance to his left rear, Tori might be able to use *Harai-goshi* effectively—but it is not easy. Better for him to lower his body, by bending his left knee, and attack with *Tai-otoshi* or *Maki-komi,* He will have to use powerful thrust to his left with his hips and arms to overcome Uke's change of balance, and he may find it more effective to thrust Uke in a circular movement round his own right hip. As Uke has taken his right leg back, the thrust round Tori's hip will be direct to his front (Fig. 162). The illustration shows *Maki-komi*—the winding version—in which Tori's right arm retains its position round Uke's right arm.

If Uke escapes by throwing his weight and balance directly to his rear, possibly bending his knees as he does so (neither good nor effective judo), Tori might try *Harai-goshi*—which may not succeed if Uke has broken contact and will most certainly fail if he

FIG 162

has bent his knees. But an attack with *Tai-otoshi*, *Uchi-mata* or *Maki-komi* could be successful.

Change of Direction of Attack

Should Uke transfer his balance to his left rear, Tori can pivot a little to his right on his left foot—turning to face Uke as he does so. At the same time, he will bring his right leg between Uke's legs and attack Uke's left leg with *O-uchi-gari*.

If Uke resists by bending his knees and leaning back, Tori can pivot to his right on his left foot and bring his right leg outside Uke's right leg to attack with *O-soto-gari*. It will assist his throw if Tori can drive his right shoulder into Uke's right chest as he attacks. He might also be able to hop in towards Uke on his left foot during the throw to improve his position.

Possible Counters to Ippon-seoi-nage

This throw is liable to rear counters. Also possible are *Uki-goshi* and *O-goshi* to the left, and side Sacrifice throws such as *Yoko-gake* and *Ura-nage*.

MOROTE-SEOI-NAGE—TWO SIDED SHOULDER THROW

Opportunity

When Uke is fairly upright or leaning slightly forward.

Timing

When Tori is able to make close contact with Uke.

The Throw

This is, in my opinion, a far more powerful throw than *Ippon-seoi-nage* but more difficult to perform.

Tori brings his right foot close to the toes of Uke's right foot, bending his right knee and breaking Uke's balance to his front and upwards as he does so. Tori must keep his right elbow quite close to his side (Fig. 163). He turns to his left, pivoting on his right foot, and turns his right wrist upwards—just as if he were aiming a right hook at the left side of Uke's jaw. As he turns, Tori's left arm continues to

FIG 163   FIG 164

lift Uke and pull him to his front while his right arm thrusts Uke upwards and to his front. It is essential that the pull should be maintained directly to Uke's front—for even a slight deviation to the side would enable Uke to escape. Tori continues the turn until his left hip drives into Uke's body: and it is now that Tori's right elbow, which has been kept close to his body, is brought up into Uke's right armpit (Fig. 164). This not only assists the lift but also makes it difficult for Uke to escape round Tori's right side. The throw is completed by Tori continuing to turn, thrusting his hips—particularly his left hip—back into Uke's body and driving forward, to Uke's front, and upwards with his arms.

It should be noted that Tori must not dip or lower his right shoulder in the early stages of the throw in order to bring it under Uke's arm and obtain close contact. The left shoulder might be lowered more than the right, but the ideal is for both shoulders to be lowered equally by bending the knees.

Variations

If Tori is shorter than Uke

Tori can concentrate on upward and forward thrust, as shown in Figure 163, moving his body in under Uke's arms.

If Tori is taller than Uke

Tori would be unwise to attempt the throw if he were much taller than Uke. If the difference is slight, however, Tori would combine his forward and upwards pull with a powerful outward pull to separate Uke's arms.

Successive Attack with the Same Throw

The throw often fails because Tori is held out by Uke's arms (Fig. 165). In such a case, Tori must pull Uke forward and upwards, lowering his own body by bending his knees. Maintaining a powerful thrust to Uke's front and upwards with his arms (Fig. 166), Tori then takes a rapid series of short steps backwards until he makes the necessary contact for the throw (Fig. 167).

FIG 165

FIG 166

Change of Throw in the Same Direction

Should Uke defend by leaning backwards or pushing Tori away, Tori can slide his right leg back and attack with *Tai-otoshi*.

If Uke takes his balance and weight back to his left back corner, Tori might succeed with *Tai-otoshi*—but *Maki-komi* would be stronger. *Seoi-otoshi* would also be effective.

Uke might escape round Tori's right side only to be thrown with *Harai-goshi*, Tori sweeping as Uke moves round.

If Uke defends by bending his knees and leaning back, *Tai-otoshi* or *Maki-komi* could be effective.

Change of Direction of Attack

Should Uke defend by bending his knees and leaning back, Tori can pivot to his right on his left foot, bringing his right foot either round Uke's right foot from the outside to attack with *O-soto-gari* or round Uke's left foot from the inside for *O-uchi-gari*.

O-uchi-gari can also be used if Uke transfers his weight and balance to his left back corner: but it is possible that Uke will have turned too far for this throw to be successful. Tori may stand more chance here if he makes a big turn to his right to attack with *Tai-otoshi* to the left.

FIG 167

Possible Counters to Morote-seoi-nage

The same as those used against Ippon-seoi-nage (page 111). Additionally, *Ushiro-goshi* and *Utsuri-goshi* are possible.

SEOI-OTOSHI—BODY DROP THROW

Opportunity

When Uke is fairly upright and perhaps holding out, or when Tori is able to straighten Uke's body.

Timing

When Tori can bring Uke's balance forward, without necessarily being as close as for other shoulder throws.

The Throw

Tori pulls Uke forward and upwards and turns to his left, pivoting on his right foot. At a convenient point in his turn—probably when the turn has reached about 45°—he releases his hold on Uke's jacket with his right hand and brings his right arm under Uke's right arm, grasping Uke's sleeve with his right hand so that Uke's arm is held between Tori's forearm and upper arm. Figure 168 shows this position, and it will be obvious that since Tori does not have to get his shoulder under Uke's arm he will not need to come in as low as for *Morote-seoi-nage*. As soon as the right hand grips Uke's sleeve it pulls upwards and forwards to assist the pull of Tori's left hand, which has maintained its pull throughout. Tori continues his turn and, as it nears completion, slides his right foot outside Uke's right leg. The turn should have brought Tori into close contact with Uke from shoulder to ankle, so that the full power of Tori's body is brought into action to drive Uke to the mat over his outstretched right leg (Fig. 169). This illustration shows a slight variation in which Tori does not grip Uke's jacket with his right hand: similar to *Ippon-seoi-nage*.

FIG 168   FIG 169

Variations

If Tori is shorter than Uke

This throw is not particularly suited to the shorter man and it might be wiser of Tori to use *Ippon-seoi-nage* or *Morote-seoi-nage*.

If Tori is taller than Uke

The throw should be performed as described above. This is the ideal version for the taller man.

Successive Attack with the Same Throw

Should Uke step over Tori's outstretched right leg, Tori should nold Uke off balance, re-position his left foot and attack again.

Change of Throw in the Same Direction

Because of the powerful pull on his right, Uke is likely to attempt to ride round Tori's right side or move his left hip forward into the left side of Tori's back to check the pull. In the case of the former, Tori could sweep with a form of *Harai-goshi;* or, if Uke has his legs wide apart, Tori could move his left foot back a little and bring his right leg and hip between Uke's legs to attack with *Uchi-mata*.

If, however, Uke moves his left hip into Tori's body, Tori should move his left foot forward and, if possible, a little to his left while bending his left knee to attack with *Tai-otoshi* or a *Maki-komi* type of throw.

Change of Direction of Attack

Tori should be in close bodily contact with Uke. Therefore, if Uke resists by throwing his balance and weight back, Tori could turn a little to his right on his left foot and bring his right leg round Uke's right leg from the outside to attack with *O-soto-gari*. Or he could use *O-uchi-gari* by bringing his right leg between Uke's legs and reaping Uke's left leg.

Because of the close contact, Tori could greatly assist both of these throws by driving his right shoulder into Uke's chest as he attacks.

Possible Counters to Seoi-Otoshi

In the early stages of the throw, possible counters are *O-goshi* and *Ushiro-goshi*. Later, Sacrifice throws such as *Yoko-guruma* could be successful.

CHAPTER VIII

Sutemi-Waza – Sacrifice Techniques

These are the techniques in which Tori sacrifices his upright position in order to make his throw. If, for instance, Uke crouches and leans forward to hold Tori away, Tori has only to throw himself on his back or down on to his left side for Uke to fall over him. And this sacrifice by Tori can be developed into a graceful, powerful and extremely effective throw.

Sacrifice techniques are divided into two main classes: one in which Tori throws himself on his back—*Ma-sutemi-waza*—and the other in which he throws himself to his side—*Yoko-sutemi-waza*.

Ma-Sutemi-Waza

TOMOE-NAGE—STOMACH THROW

Opportunity

When there is a gap between Tori and Uke, caused perhaps by Uke's defensive posture or stiff arms.

Timing

As Uke pushes forward in an attempt to protect himself from a close-contact technique or can be persuaded to lean forward.

The Throw

Tori pulls Uke to his front and upwards, tending to straighten Uke and tilt him even more to his front. At the same time, Tori glides in with his left foot, replacing it on the mat between Uke's feet or as nearly so as possible without losing his balance backwards. As he moves in, Tori bends his left knee (Fig. 170), lowering himself until he is sitting close to his own left heel while bringing the sole of his right foot gently to Uke's abdomen. He should place his right foot so that

FIG 170

FIG 171

FIG 172

his toes are just below the knot of Uke's belt (Fig. 171). Tori's right foot is only a guide and *not* a lever. Having made the foot contact, Tori rolls back, maintaining his forward and upward pull and rolling Uke in a circle over him to land on the mat behind his head. Tori's foot acts as the spoke of a wheel of which Uke is the rim and Tori's right hip is the hub (Fig. 172).

There is another version of this throw in which Tori changes his direction half way through and throws Uke to his left or right at about the level of Tori's shoulder.

Variations

If Tori is shorter than Uke

This is ideal. Tori thrusts Uke's arms upwards from below, dropping himself right under Uke to make the throw.

If Tori is taller than Uke

He will have to lift powerfully from above, making up with additional lift what is lost by his inability to lower himself right under Uke.

Successive Attack with the Same Throw

Not possible.

Change of Throw in the Same Direction

If Tori fails to score a point, he can pursue Uke by turning to his side and attacking with groundwork.

Change of Direction of Attack

Should the throw fail, Tori might be able to trap Uke's leg and throw him to his rear. He would do it thus: assuming that he is on his back and has his right foot against Uke's abdomen, he brings his left foot outside Uke's right foot, placing it behind Uke's heel and pulling Uke's foot forward. He then places the sole of his right foot just below Uke's left knee and pushes. This "scissor" action will throw Uke on to his back.

Possible Counters to Tomoe-nage

It is very difficult to counter this throw, but in its early stages a rear throw such as *O-uchi-gari* or *Ko-uchi-gari* might succeed. Later, as Tori takes him over, Uke could escape by using the "butterfly" turn and then counter-attack with a hold down.

Yoko-Sutemi-Waza

YOKO-GURUMA—SIDE WHEEL

Opportunity

When Uke is in a defensive posture, perhaps holding out with stiff arms.

Timing

When Uke can be persuaded to move his right leg forward, or as he pushes with his right arm in the vicinity of Tori's left shoulder.

The Throw

Tori must position his left foot close to Uke's right foot. Then, as Uke pushes forward with his right arm or advances his right leg,

Tori bends his knees to lower his body and thrusts Uke's body upwards. As he does this, he glides his right leg along the mat in an anti-clockwise circular movement, sliding it deeply between Uke's legs. At this point, Tori drops to the mat, the withdrawal of his left hip bringing him on his left side (Fig. 173). Tori may find it helpful—and, if Uke is crouching, not too difficult—to bring his left arm round Uke's body to clasp Uke's belt at the back. His right hand can grip the front of Uke's belt. Both hands drive Uke upwards.

If the throw is attempted when Uke has his right foot back, he will be unable to turn on that foot and will be thrown on his face.

FIG 173

Variations

If Tori is shorter than Uke

He moves in under Uke's right arm, thrusting it upwards, and slides his left arm round Uke's waist in *Kata* fashion.

If Tori is Taller than Uke

Any attempt to make close contact will almost certainly be checked by Uke's right arm. To overcome this, Tori can drive Uke's right arm outwards, stepping inside it to bring his left foot outside Uke's right and placing his left arm round Uke's waist. He may have to bring his left arm over Uke's right shoulder to hold the back of Uke's belt or jacket—but this is not really the most satisfactory way since it makes it harder for Tori to keep on balance when lowering the hip and bringing the right foot into position to effect the throw.

Successive Attack with the Same Throw

Once committed to this throw, a second attempt is not possible.

Change of Throw in the Same Direction

If Uke defends by bringing his left leg forward—and provided he advances his left leg before Tori is fully committed—Tori can turn to his right by taking his right leg back and sitting down close to his own left heel. As he does so, he must slide his right foot along the mat, stretching it out in front of Uke's leg and turning Uke to his left front. This would be a left-handed *Yoko-gake*.

Change of Direction of Attack

Uke might well defend by throwing his weight backwards. In such case—and, again, provided he is not fully committed—Tori can pivot to his right on his right foot, bringing his left hip forward and sliding his left foot along the mat so that his left leg is outstretched behind Uke's heels (Fig. 174). At the same time, he uses his hands in a circular motion—his left taking Uke back and down, his right driving Uke upwards and back over Tori's outstretched left leg.

FIG 174

Possible Counters to Yoko-Guruma

O-uchi-gari or *Ko-uchi-gari*, as for *Tomoe-nage*.

YOKO-GAKE—SIDE BODY THROW

Opportunity

When Uke is in a defensive posture and has been persuaded to advance his right leg.

Timing

As Uke brings his balance over his right leg.

The Throw

Tori pulls Uke to his front and upwards and, bending his right knee to lower his body, steps round to Uke's left side with his right foot, turning it towards his left as he does so (Fig. 175A). His right knee must be bent quite deeply. He then turns to his left, withdrawing his left hip and sliding his left foot out along the mat so that his left leg is stretched straight out in front of Uke's left foot (Fig. 175B) as he drops on his left side to the mat (Fig. 176). No physical contact need be made, other than the original hand grip, but Tori must continue to turn until he drops to the mat.

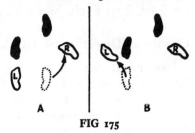

FIG 175

FIG 176

Variations

If Tori is shorter than Uke

Tori will thrust Uke's arms upwards from below, moving under Uke's arms to achieve the position shown in Figure 175B.

If Tori is taller than Uke

The lift will be from above, and Tori can make the throw from longer range.

Successive Attack with the Same Throw

Once fully committed to this throw, a second attempt is not likely to succeed.

Change of Throw in the Same Direction

Tori might be able to turn the throw into *Tomoe-nage* by turning on to his back.

Change of Direction of Attack

Virtually impossible.

Possible Counters to Yoko-gake

This is difficult to counter, but it might be possible to use *Ko-soto-gari* as the throw commences. If Uke can step over Tori's left foot he can produce a very powerful *Yoko-gake* of his own to the left.

YOKO-WAKARE—SIDE SEPARATION

Opportunity

When Uke is in a defensive position and has his right leg advanced.

Timing

As Uke brings his balance over his right leg.

The Throw

Tori draws Uke forward and upwards and turns to his left on his left foot, gliding his right foot across in front of Uke. As Tori's left leg straightens he drops to the mat in front of Uke, sliding his right foot along the mat so that his right leg stretches beside his

FIG 177

left (Fig. 177). The 'thrust of Tori's arms, backed by the power generated by the turn of his body, drives Uke to the mat over Tori's legs.

This is a stronger throw than *Yoko-gake* because Tori is able to put the whole power of his body behind the thrust of his arms.

Variations

If Tori is shorter than Uke

His task is made easier by being able to drive Uke's arms upwards and to his front from below.

If Tori is taller than Uke

He will tend to lift his opponent from above, but as he drops to the mat he must change this to a thrust from below without pulling Uke downwards.

Successive Attack with the Same Throw

A second attempt will not be possible.

Change of Throw in the Same Direction

Once committed, Tori cannot change his throw.

Change of Direction of Attack

Once committed, Tori cannot change direction.

Possible Counters to Yoko-wakare

Early in the attack, *Ko-soto-gari* is possible. Later, a counter with this same throw—*Yoko-wakare*—could succeed.

CHAPTER IX

The Unorthodox in Judo Throws

It can quite often be the unorthodox, and therefore unexpected move which helps to win that all-important point in a contest. This is not to say that discipline may go by the board, but merely that a throw might be successfully attempted in circumstances other than those which have been taught as ideal.

For example, the beginner is taught to attempt *Tsurikomi-ashi* as his opponent advances his right foot—and this is something of which all judomen are wary. It will be found, however, that this throw—or, perhaps, *Hiza-guruma*—can be made when Uke takes his right leg back, the attack still being made with Tori's left foot against Uke's right leg. Because Uke will not be anticipating it, the throw could well succeed.

Sometimes Tori can use his arm in a throw which is usually made with the hips or legs, and such a move could be used as a continuation of *Ippon-seoi-nage*. Let us say that Tori attacks with *Ippon-seoi-nage* and, although he completes his turn, finds that he is unable to make his throw. Provided he is still on balance, he holds his position and continues to pull Uke forward and upwards, maintaining his grip with his right hand on Uke's right sleeve. But he releases his left hand hold and slides his left arm down to his left and between Uke's legs to grip Uke's left trouser leg at about the back of the knee (Fig. 178). With a turn of the hips to his left, the pull of his right hand and the upward lift with his left, Tori throws Uke over his back to the mat.

Generally speaking, it is bad judo to defend by grabbing an opponent's trousers and lifting his leg to effect some sort of counter—but a smooth and rapid movement of this kind can succeed. An example is a counter to *Tsurikomi-ashi*. The attack is made on the defender's right, the left leg being stretched out to make the throw. The defender manages to brace himself sufficiently to check the throw and catches the attacker's trouser leg with his right hand. He then pulls the attacker's left leg forward and upwards, bringing his own left leg between the attacker's legs and reaping the right leg away to counter the throw with *O-uchi-gari*.

When and how to attempt something a little out of the ordinary is naturally a matter for the discretion of the contestant. His own common sense, experience and ability will be his guide, and I do not feel there is any need for me to elaborate on the theme. It did seem, however, that before turning from throws to holds and locks there should be this brief reminder of the importance of the element of surprise. The keen contest man will surely find his own methods of turning the unexpected move to his advantage.

FIG 178

CHAPTER X

Katame-Waza – Holding Techniques and Locks

Katame-waza include *Osaekomi-waza* (holding down), *Shime-waza* (neck locks) and *Kansetsu-waza* (locks on the arm).

This branch of judo is only too often neglected, and seldom is it given the position of importance it deserves. One of the reasons for this is lack of mat space—and there is no gainsaying that one pair engaged in groundwork in the middle of the mat makes any other practice impossible. But this is not an insurmountable problem. Groundwork enthusiasts should practise before the bulk of club members arrive or after the others have gone: and clubs should organise special ground-work sessions. Another reason for skirting around *Katame-waza* is the belief held by some that the advantage always lies with the bigger and stronger man. Within certain obvious limits, this is a fallacy. Ground-work requires no greater strength than *Tachi-waza*, depending rather on skill and relaxation. Tori, though he might be somewhat stronger than Uke, cannot maintain a hold-down if he is tense, cannot strangle if his arms are stiff, and cannot apply armlocks if he fails to control Uke.

As to whether groundwork is easier than standing techniques, my answer is unquestionably *no*! Both have exactly the same basic principles with regard to freedom of movement of the hips, control over the opponent, and relaxation. And imagination and ingenuity are called upon to develop an opponent's slightest error into a decisive lock or hold. Locks, it should be remembered, can be applied from almost any position.

OSAEKOMI-WAZA—HOLDING TECHNIQUES, COMMENCING GROUNDWORK

Contest Rules

It is forbidden to drag an opponent down with the intention of commencing groundwork. A genuine attempt at a throw must be made. It is also forbidden to apply a lock standing and use that lock to pull the opponent down to the mat. The rules state:

1. When a contestant brings his opponent to the mat with a technique which is not sufficiently clean to obtain a point, he may follow to the ground in order to commence groundwork. This is the usual method of commencing groundwork.

2. When the attacker falls in attempting a throw, the contestant attacked can follow him to the ground and commence groundwork.

3. Standing arm locks and neck locks are allowed, but it is not permitted to bring the opponent down to the mat by means of such a lock. If, however, Uke drops to the mat—perhaps to his knees—in an effort to escape, Tori can follow to the mat and commence groundwork, maintaining the lock originally applied if he wishes to do so.

A Hold at the Edge of the Mat

Once the referee has called "*Osaekomi*" ("Holding"), a deliberate escape over the edge of the mat is forbidden. Should the contestants reach the edge of the mat, the referee will call "*Somo-mama*" ("Keep still") and the contestants will be pulled back into the centre of the mat.

Hold-Down

Osaekomi is applied when the opponent is held on his back in a technical hold for a period of 30 seconds—"technical hold" meaning having the opponent under control with one limb pinned. Such a hold maintained for more than 25 seconds but less than 30 seconds scores *Waza-ari* (near point).

KESA-GATAME—SCARF HOLD-DOWN

This is the ideal follow-up to an attempted throw which has brought Uke down but failed to score. It demonstrates the value of maintaining control over Uke.

As Uke reaches the mat, Tori—still standing beside him—pulls his sleeve upwards, bringing his right foot against the right side of Uke's body. Tori's right knee should be well bent, so that his shin presses against Uke's chest and holds him securely on the mat (Fig. 179). Maintaining the upward pull on Uke's arm, Tori drops to the mat with his right hip close to Uke's right side, sliding his right leg down Uke's body as he drops. He can place his right hand on the mat at Uke's left side to prevent himself actually falling on Uke. As he reaches the mat, Tori spreads his legs, throwing the right leg forward and the left leg back. His legs should be really well spread, with his right knee close to Uke's right ear. He continues his pull on Uke's arm in order to control him, pulling it across his own body so that it is pinned between his arm, abdomen and right hip

FIG 179

FIG 180

(Fig. 180). Then, as quickly as possible, Tori brings his right arm under Uke's neck and clasps his jacket behind the right shoulder or grips his own right trouser leg near the knee (Fig. 181).

In the final position, Tori presses the "sharp" side of his

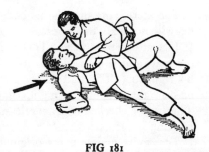

FIG 181

body—his ribs—down against the side of Uke's body in a cutting action. This presses the air out of Uke's lungs, making the hold more exhausting and therefore more effective. It will be more effective still if it can be applied as Uke breathes out, so that the pressure is brought to bear against empty lungs.

Variations

Tori may lean his body forward, with his head down to the right side of Uke's head (Fig. 182). This prevents Uke from pressing on Tori's jaw in an effort to escape. In my opinion, however, the advantage of avoiding a counter is outweighed by the fact that the curve of Tori's body forward releases the pressure on Uke's body maintained in the first form of the hold.

FIG 182

Maintaining the Hold against Opposition

The more Tori spreads his body the stronger the hold will be. For he will need all the leverage he can get to check Uke's struggles. If Uke attempts to sit up, Tori resists by pressing his left foot against the mat; and if Uke tries to roll backwards, Tori presses down with his right foot. The pull on the right arm prevents Uke from turning on his right side, but he might attempt to roll Tori over to his left side. This can be checked by Tori releasing his right hand for a moment and pushing it against the mat at Uke's left side (Fig. 183).

Tori must maintain his original position relative to his opponent

FIG 183

throughout. This means that if Uke moves around in his struggles Tori must move with him, always keeping his right knee close to Uke's right ear and his legs well spread.

Change of Hold

If Uke manages to get his body under Tori and threatens to roll Tori over him to the mat at his left side, Tori can check the move by pivoting on his hips, taking his right hip back and his left hip forward (Fig. 184) until he is almost face down on the mat, thrusting Uke again on to his back. The same tactics can be used if Uke manages to loosen Tori's hold, enabling Tori to renew the hold.

If Uke succeeds in freeing his right arm and commences to pull his right hip and shoulder away, turning on his right side, Tori can change the hold to *Kami-shiho-gatame* by pivoting on his hips, throwing his right leg back and left leg forward, and turning on to his face, bringing his left arm under Uke's neck to hold the jacket at Uke's left shoulder. He must then, as soon as he can, bring his right hand

FIG 184

131

between Uke's legs from above and grasp the back of Uke's belt or the back of his jacket as high as possible.

If Uke manages to free his right hand and pushes at Tori's jaw or chest, Tori can change his hold to *Kata-gatame* by pushing Uke's arm across his own neck.

Arm Locks obtainable from the Hold

Should Uke free his right arm, instead of attempting *Kata-gatame* Tori could pull the arm outwards, straightening it and bringing his left knee over the wrist or forearm. By holding the arm down with his left leg or left arm and raising his right thigh, Tori can apply an effective arm lock (Fig. 185). Uke's arm might equally well be pushed upwards and held under Tori's right leg, the lock being applied by the combined action of Tori's right leg and left arm.

An alternative lock on Uke's right arm can be applied if he straightens it in an attempt to push Tori away. Tori grips Uke's wrist or sleeve and pulls the arm straight and upwards. At the same time, he brings his left leg forward—a hip movement—and places it outside Uke's right arm and across his neck. Then Tori falls back, pulling the arm straight, and applies a form of *Ju-ji-gatame*.

If Uke pushes Tori away with his left arm, pressing up against Tori's right shoulder or jaw, Tori should grip Uke's left wrist with his left hand. Then, by pivoting on his hips so that he turns face down, he can force Uke's arm on to the mat to apply *Ude-garami*. Or, in the same situation, he could bring his left leg over Uke's neck, placing his foot on the mat at the left side of Uke's neck, to pull Uke's arm out straight and upwards while coming to the kneel on his right knee. He would follow this up by pressing against Uke's elbow, straightening his own body in order to stretch Uke's arm in *Ude-gatame*.

FIG 185

Note

It will be seen that everything in connection with *Kesa-gatame* requires hip movement. The judoman must therefore have full flexibility and freedom of the hips throughout.

KATA-GATAME—SHOULDER HOLD

Uke is on his back, with Tori at his right side. Perhaps because Uke straightens his right arm in an attempt to hold him off, Tori is able to push the arm to Uke's left so that it lies across Uke's neck. Tori immediately drops face down on the mat at Uke's right side, his right arm round Uke's neck and his head pressing against Uke's right arm to hold it in position across Uke's neck. Tori then brings his left arm under Uke's neck from the right and clasps his own hands. He is still face down, balanced on his toes and with his hips raised. His left leg is out to his left and his right leg is close to Uke's right foot. To apply the lock Tori tightens the pressure of his arms round Uke's neck and against his right arm and, by thrusting from his toes, presses his weight forward against Uke's right shoulder (Fig. 186).

FIG 186

Variations

There are none of any importance.

Maintaining the Hold against Opposition

This is a very difficult hold to break, and Uke would have to devote his efforts to forcing a gap between himself and Tori's head and right shoulder to free his own right arm. Tori must therefore maintain his thrust against Uke's shoulder continuously. The thrust is down towards the mat and not across Uke, to prevent Uke attempting a backward roll out of the hold.

Change of Hold

The changes are very like those for *Kesa-gatame*. If Uke frees his right arm, Tori can change to *Kesa-gatame* by bringing his right leg forward and immediately pinning Uke's right arm. Or he could bring his right arm between Uke's legs to grasp the back of his belt or jacket and apply *Yoko-shiho-gatame*. He should not find it difficult to bring his right leg over Uke's body to take up an astride position.

Arm Locks obtainable from the Hold

A lock against Uke's right arm is difficult, but *Ude-garami* and *Ude-gatame* are possible against his left arm.

KUZURE-KESA-GATAME—BROKEN SCARF HOLD

The only difference between this hold and *Kesa-gatame* is the use made by Tori of his right arm. Here he passes it under Uke's left armpit and places his hand, palm down, on the mat close to Uke's left shoulder and in line with his head (Fig. 187). It will help if Uke's left arm can be pushed a little above the level of his shoulder. In one respect this is the stronger hold of the two, in that Tori has his right arm free to support him should Uke attempt to roll him over, stretching it wide and using it as a brace (Fig. 188).

FIG 187

134

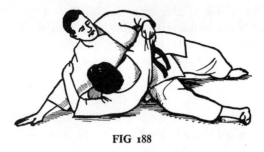

FIG 188

Variations, Maintaining the Hold against Opposition, Change of Hold and *Arm Locks obtainable from the Hold* are all covered by the information given under these headings for *Kesa-gatame* (pages 130 to 132).

YOKO-SHIHO-GATAME—SIDE FOUR QUARTER HOLD

Many judomen find this a difficult hold to maintain. The opportunity to attempt it occurs when Uke is on his back and Tori is on the ground at his right. Tori brings his left hand over Uke's head, reaching round and under his left shoulder to grasp his jacket at the left side. If possible, he should grip Uke's belt. Tori passes his right hand between Uke's legs and grips the back of his jacket as high up as he can (Fig. 189). As the diagram shows, Tori adopts a face-down position, spreading his legs wide apart and pressing his hips down on to the mat at Uke's right side. His head and chest press down on to Uke's body.

Tori must take care not to get his body too far across Uke's. Any tendency to balance on his opponent will endanger his position, making it easy for Uke to roll him off. Similarly, it is important that Tori maintains the pressure of his hips on the mat. If he should raise

FIG 189

his hips, Uke would be able to throw him off or escape to his left.

To complete the hold, Tori pulls Uke down on to the mat and in towards his own hips—his hands pinning Uke's left side and his hips pinning Uke's right side.

Variations

Tori could bring his left hand *under* Uke's head to hold the back of his jacket below the left shoulder. In all other respects, the hold would be achieved as above mentioned.

A second variation is to draw up the knees close to Uke's side. In this case, Tori's hips will not be on the mat but should be pressed downwards.

Maintaining the Hold against Opposition

Tori must keep his hips down on the mat and pull Uke down and towards him throughout the hold. If Uke moves around in his struggles, Tori must follow him to maintain their relative positions—but he must move from his toes, pressing them into the mat and keeping his knees off the mat. If Tori presses his knees into the mat, his hips will automatically lift and the hold will be broken.

Change of Hold

Tori can change to *Kami-shiho-gatame* by withdrawing his right hand from between Uke's legs and grasping Uke's belt at his right side. Then, holding Uke firmly, he moves round so that his hips are on the mat above Uke's head, with his legs spread wide.

A change to *Kuzure-kami-shiho-gatame* is equally simple. Tori slips his left hand over Uke's left arm, having released his hold on Uke's belt, and brings his arm over Uke's arm and under his shoulders to grip Uke's collar as far to Uke's right as possible. Alternatively, he could grip the jacket material below Uke's right shoulder. Tori then withdraws his right hand from between Uke's legs and grips Uke's belt at his right side. As he does this, he moves his body round so that his weight bears down on Uke's right shoulder: but he must keep his hips on the mat as he moves.

The sequence of hand movements here is interchangeable. Which hand Tori moves first will depend upon the action required to defeat Uke's efforts to escape.

Arm Locks obtainable from the Hold

Because Tori has no control over Uke's body, he will find it very difficult to lock Uke's right arm. If Uke manages to free his right arm and succeeds in pushing Tori upwards, Tori might be able to grip the arm and rise to his knees. He could then, by bringing his left leg over Uke's neck, apply *Ju-ji-gatame:* but it would be a cumbersome movement.

Uke's left arm, being comparatively free, could get into trouble should he use it to push Tori away. *Ude-garami* would be applied if Uke pushes at Tori's left shoulder or his head, Tori gripping Uke's left wrist with his left hand and thrusting Uke's arm flat on the mat so that the wrist is above Uke's shoulder to apply the lock.

In the same situation, instead of using *Ude-garami*, Tori can allow Uke a certain amount of success with his left-hand thrust, rising with him as he pushes so that Uke's left arm is fully stretched upwards. Tori rises to his knees as Uke pushes, kneeling at Uke's right side and bringing his hands against the outside of Uke's elbow, perhaps bringing his left leg round Uke's head to pin him. To apply the lock, Tori pulls Uke's elbow inwards and upwards, thrusting his hips forward at the same time. This is *Ude-gatame.*

KAMI-SHIHO-GATAME—UPPER FOUR QUARTER HOLD

This hold is applied when Uke is on his back and Tori is positioned above or close to his head. Tori passes his arms round Uke's arms and grasps Uke's belt at his sides, holding fairly far back on the belt so that his hands are close to the mat. He then drops his body on to the mat, with his knees drawn up towards Uke's shoulders but as wide-spread as possible, and his head pressing on to Uke's body as high up Uke's body as possible (Fig. 190). Tori presses his hips down towards the mat although there is no actual contact.

FIG 190

Variations

Tori takes the same hand-hold round Uke's arms, gripping his belt at mat level and pressing his head as high up Uke's body as possible. This time, however, he

FIG 191

throws his legs straight back and spreads them wide apart, the weight of his hips dropping firmly on the mat (Fig. 191) and giving him great stability.

Tori could make the hand-hold inside Uke's arms (Fig. 192) and then continue as described above.

It should be noted that in this hold and its variations Tori's head must be as close to Uke's chest as possible, with the top of his head above Uke's belt. A lower position will bring Tori's hips on to Uke's head rather than the mat, greatly weakening the hold.

FIG 192

Maintaining the Hold against Opposition

Tori must pull upwards, not only tightening the hold but also restricting Uke's breathing and consequently weakening his efforts to escape.

To free himself, Uke may move round so that his body is in line with one of Tori's legs and attempt to roll him over in that direction. And it is to prevent this that Tori should keep his legs spread as widely as possible to either side and maintain his upward pull on Uke's belt.

Another manoeuvre Uke might employ is to turn himself almost sideways to Tori. With good timing and keen judgment, he can then remove Tori completely by rolling him across his own body in a forward roll. To counter this, Tori must move with Uke and keep his legs spread equally to either side of Uke's body, pulling Uke upwards with his grip on the belt and pressing his own hips well down on to the mat to continue the hold as already explained. Tori must move round by pressing his toes—not his knees—on the mat.

Change of Hold

If Uke's struggles begin to break Tori's hold, Tori can move round Uke's side—let us say, in this instance, his left side—and, by bringing his left arm between Uke's legs, can change the hold to *Yoko-shiho-gatame*.

If Uke succeeds in lifting his left shoulder and freeing his right hip and side, Tori brings his left arm under Uke's left armpit and grasps the back of Uke's collar or jacket, moving his body round to his left so that his hips are above Uke's left shoulder and pinning it firmly to the mat. This is *Kuzure-kami-shiho-gatame*.

Arm Locks obtainable from the Hold

It is very difficult for Tori to apply a lock while still retaining control of Uke's body. The opportunity to attempt one might occur when Uke, in his efforts to escape, succeeds in moving round so that Tori is more at his side—rather in the position adopted for *Yoko-shiho-gatame*. And indeed Tori can, in such a position, attempt the locks described for that hold.

KUZURE-KAMI-SHIHO-GATAME—BROKEN UPPER FOUR QUARTER HOLD

With Uke on his back, Tori positions himself above or near his opponent's head. He then brings his left arm over and round Uke's left arm, passing his hand under Uke's left armpit and shoulder to grip the collar of Uke's jacket as far to Uke's right as possible—or to grip the back of Uke's jacket at the back of Uke's right shoulder (Fig. 193). It may not be possible for Tori to drive his left hand straight under Uke's shoulder and into position at once, but if he manages to get it in the general area it will be sufficient to immobilise Uke. Then, during Uke's struggles, Tori can take a more permanent hold. In any event, Tori's right hand passes either under or over Uke's right shoulder to hold Uke's belt well down with his hand close to the mat. Both of Tori's hands pull upwards, towards Uke's head—thus pinning Uke's arms—and Tori drops his hips on to the mat above Uke's left shoulder. In doing this, Tori spreads his legs and presses his head and chest down onto Uke's shoulder and chest (Fig. 193).

There are two things to particularly note. One is that Tori lies at an angle to Uke's body, pressing his hips on the mat over the shoulder

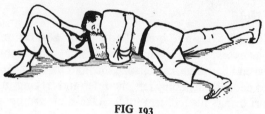

FIG 193

under which he has passed his arm. The other is that Tori must not place his head too far down Uke's body, with the danger of placing his hips on Uke's shoulder instead of the mat and so weakening the hold.

Variations

There are no major variations.

Maintaining the Hold against Opposition

As for *Kami-shiho-gatame*, with Tori maintaining the relative position between himself and Uke if Uke moves around. Uke's movements should be restricted by the upward pull of Tori's arms. An attempt to roll Tori sideways is checked by pressure of the appropriate foot by Tori—pressing, of course, from the toes. Efforts to backward-roll out of the hold are prevented by the downward pressure from Tori's head.

Change of Hold

Tori can change to *Yoko-shiho-gatame*, particularly to the side to which he is already inclined.

It is also possible to change to *Ushiro-kesa-gatame* (Reverse Scarf Hold)—a full explanation of which follows on page 142. When Tori is pinning Uke's left shoulder, it is hardly necessary for him to change his hand or arm position. Only his body has to be moved, pivoting on his hips to bring his right leg and thigh forward so that he is sitting on his right thigh at Uke's left side. The position is similar to *Kesa-gatame*, except that Tori is now sitting the other way round. Tori's right forearm should be brought against Uke's right side, with the elbow pressed up into Uke's armpit (Fig. 194). His left hand is removed from behind Uke to grip Uke's left sleeve on the underside, close to the armpit, pressing Uke's arm between Tori's left arm, abdomen and right thigh (Fig. 195).

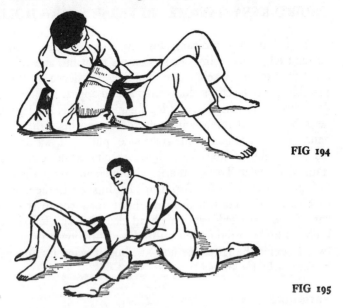

FIG 194

FIG 195

Arm Locks obtainable from the Hold

Although these are limited, Tori's hold on Uke's left arm provides some opportunity. Tori maintains his grip on Uke's sleeve with his left hand and pulls it hard to his left—that is, at right-angles to Uke's body—pivoting on his right hip and throwing his left leg over Uke's body. His right leg is brought along the left side of Uke's body. By pulling Uke's arm outwards, to straighten it, and lifting his hips, Tori applies the lock (Fig. 196).

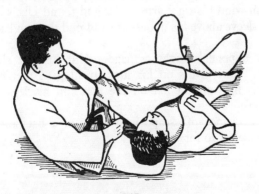

FIG 196

USHIRO-KESA-GATAME—REVERSE SCARF HOLD

Applied from a position close to Uke's shoulder, when Uke is on his back, Tori reclines or sits on his right hip and thigh and grips the left sleeve of Uke's jacket, holding the sleeve on the underside, possibly closer to Uke's elbow than would appear in Figure 195. As he does this, he throws his right leg forward and his left leg back so that he is balanced at three points: each foot and his right hip. His right hand grips Uke's belt at his right side, pulling upwards and pressing his right elbow into Uke's right armpit; while Uke's left arm is trapped between Tori's left arm, abdomen and right thigh—as shown in Figures 194 and 195. Tori drops his hips on to the mat and not on to Uke's body. He can drop his body forward, so that his back is curved—and relaxed—with his head close to Uke's left side; or he can keep his body upright—but still relaxed—hollowing his back. Of the two, I prefer the latter method . . . but, if using it, Tori will have to beware of Uke's knees.

Variations

These are mainly in respect of Tori's left-hand hold, which can vary from the armpit to the end of the sleeve: a matter of personal preference.

Maintaining the Hold against Opposition

Tori must retain his hold on and control over Uke's arms. The hold on the left arm is strong, so Uke is likely to attempt to raise the right side of his body. Tori can counter this by pressing Uke downwards with his head. If, nevertheless, Uke's lift becomes powerful, Tori can wind his right arm under and round Uke's right arm to hold Uke's sleeve above his upper arm and pull the arm back on to the mat.

A strong opponent might manage to lift his left shoulder. To counter this, Tori pivots on his hips, turning so that he faces the mat with his hips almost flat on the mat and his legs well spread out (Fig. 197).

Uke's best chance of escape is by way of a backward roll, and Tori must be alert to forestall this.

FIG 197

Change of Hold

If Uke commences to lift his right shoulder, threatening to pull his left hip and shoulder away, Tori thrusts him back by pivoting with his hips in a turn that brings his hips flat on the mat. He brings his left hand between Uke's legs to hold the back of Uke's jacket or belt as high up his body as possible. With his right hand, he releases Uke's belt to take hold of the back of Uke's jacket below his right shoulder—changing the hold to *Yoko-shiho-gatame*.

If Uke manages to lift his left shoulder or commences to sit up, Tori pivots on his hips to turn face down on the mat, moving so that his hips drop on the mat above Uke's left shoulder. His right hand retains its hold on Uke's belt; his left hand slips under Uke's shoulders to grip the back of Uke's collar or jacket behind the right shoulder. This is *Kuzure-kami-shiho-gatame*.

Tori can change to *Kami-shiho-gatame* very easily by moving round until he is pressing down on Uke's left shoulder. His right hand hold will not alter, and his left hand will have to move only the few inches from Uke's left sleeve to the left side of his belt.

Arm Locks obtainable from the Hold

If Uke manages to free his left arm, Tori can grip his wrist and push the arm down under his own left leg, applying the lock by holding Uke's wrist and forearm down with his leg and lifting Uke's elbow with his left arm or right thigh.

Should Uke's right arm become troublesome, Tori can pivot on his hips to bring himself face down across Uke, pushing Uke's right arm down on the mat with his own right hand and bringing his left hand under Uke's right upper arm to apply *Ude-garame*.

TATE-SHIHO-GATAME—VERTICAL OR LENGTHWISE FOUR QUARTER HOLD

The opportunity to apply this hold occurs when Uke is lying on his back with Tori astride him. Tori brings his right arm over Uke's left shoulder and down across his back to grip Uke's belt at his back or right side. His left arm moves under Uke's right armpit and he grips Uke's collar as far to Uke's left as possible. Figure 198 shows Uke sitting up, in order to clearly illustrate Tori's hold. With this achieved, Tori presses inwards with his arms towards Uke's head, thrusting his body upwards and bringing his head down on to the mat to the left of Uke's head (Fig. 199). He completes the hold by tucking his feet under Uke's thighs.

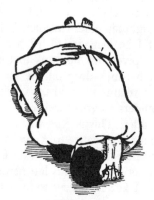

FIG 198   FIG 199

Variations

Variations to the holds of the arms are many: a matter of convenience at the time. The only essential is to control Uke's right arm.

Maintaining the Hold against Opposition

Because of the close bodily contact, every move Uke makes will immediately affect Tori. Should Uke bridge his body strongly, Tori will be lifted from the mat and will need to maintain the upward thrust which locks Uke's shoulders. Any effort to roll him off can be checked by Tori thrusting out whichever leg will stabilise him.

Change of Hold

It is not easy to change from this hold to another. However, if Uke seriously weakens Tori's hold to his right, Tori can bring his right hip over Uke's body and adopt *Kesa-gatame* or *Kata-gatame*, changing the position of his right hand as he moves. He will, of course, have to change his left hand hold to control Uke's right arm as quickly as possible.

Yoko-shiho-gatame is a better hold to change to when Tori has to move to Uke's left. Tori brings his left leg across Uke's body, placing his hips on the mat at Uke's left side and ensuring that his legs are well spread. At the same time, he brings his left arm between Uke's legs to grip the back of his belt or jacket as far up his back as possible.

Arm Locks obtainable from the Hold

If Uke frees his right arm, Tori can bring his right arm over Uke's body to grip Uke's right wrist and pin it to the mat, at the same time bringing his left leg across Uke's body so that his hips are on the mat at Uke's left side. He must then immediately bring his left arm under Uke's right upper arm to apply *Ude-garami*.

Ude-gatame is also possible, with Tori taking up a kneeling position at Uke's side.

The arm crush could be used, as could *Ude-hishige-ju-ji-gatame*. The former would be achieved as follows. Tori brings his left arm over and round Uke's right arm so that his forearm comes under Uke's upper arm and the lower part of Uke's arm projects from under Tori's left armpit (Fig. 200). At this stage, in order to maintain control, Tori could hold the upper part of Uke's right sleeve. Tori at once turns to fall on to his back at Uke's right side, bringing his left knee further up Uke's right side and close in to

FIG 200

him. His right leg remains across Uke's body to hold him down. He
then clasps his own hands so that the sharp thumb-side of his left
lower arm presses upwards against Uke's biceps (Fig. 201). To apply
the lock, Tori holds Uke down with his right leg and presses
upwards with his left forearm.

FIG 201

CHAPTER XI

Kansetsu-Waza – Arm Locking Techniques

Here are the rules governing *Kansetsu-waza*.

1. *Kansetsu-waza* may be applied standing, but it is forbidden to apply a lock standing and drag the opponent down to the mat with it.
2. If the opponent goes to the ground in an attempt to escape from a lock applied in a standing position, it is permissible to continue that lock on the ground.
3. It is forbidden to apply *Kansetsu-waza* to any joint except the elbow. Any form of groundwork which applies pressure against the spine or neck is forbidden.
4. Should a contestant be on his back with his opponent in a position to pick him up, it is forbidden for the contestant on the mat to apply *Kansetsu-waza* (Fig. 202). It is possible—in theory, at least—to apply an arm lock against an opponent on the ground whenever he moves his elbow away from his side.

Junior Contests

Kansetsu-waza are not allowed in junior contests and should not be taught to juniors.

Leverage Applied to Arm Locks

The principle of leverage applies as much to arm locks as it does to throws. In the case of throws, of course, leverage is assisted by the momentum of the attack. Tori must therefore use other means of

FIG 202

bringing maximum power into
play when applying an arm lock,
as in the following example.

Tori applies *Ude-garami* to
Uke's left arm from Uke's right
side. Uke pushes away with his
left arm (Fig. 203), and Tori
grasps Uke's left wrist and
attempts to drive Uke's arm down
flat on the mat. Uke bends his left
arm and turns it a little so that he
is able to resist. Now, instead of
fighting Uke's resistance with his
left arm, Tori brings his right

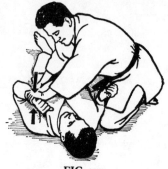

FIG 203

hand over and grips Uke's left sleeve at the elbow (Fig. 204), hollowing
his back and driving his hips forward to apply the whole power of
his body against Uke's arm sideways.

FIG 204

UDE-HISHIGI-JU-JI-GATAME—STRAIGHT ARM LOCK WITH THE THIGHS

Used against a straight arm, this is the basis of several locks. The
basic form of the lock is applied from beside an opponent who is
on his back on the mat. For instance, Tori might have brought Uke
to the mat but not sufficiently cleanly to score. He is still holding Uke's
right sleeve and now he pulls it firmly upwards, stretching Uke's arm.
At the same time, he brings his right foot close to Uke's right side. By
bending his right knee so that his shin presses Uke downwards, Tori
can completely control Uke (Fig. 205). Still pulling Uke's arm

148

upwards, Tori lowers his body by sitting close to his own right heel—at the same time bringing his left foot round the top of Uke's head so that as he sinks to his heel his left leg is stretched across Uke's neck (Fig. 206). Tori's trunk is kept upright throughout. He may grip Uke's right wrist—but if the wrist or his own hand is damp with perspiration it might not be effective. Alternatively, he could grip Uke's right sleeve first and transfer to the wrist later. But at this stage it is really sufficient for the pull to be applied to the sleeve.

FIG 205

Tori now lowers his back to the mat, his best position being at a little more than 90° to Uke's body, angled towards Uke's head. And he continues pulling Uke's arm straight out, this time towards his own head. It is at this point, when he is lying back, that Tori must grip Uke's right wrist, turning Uke's arm so that his hand is thumb uppermost (Fig. 207). Immediately he achieves this, Tori brings his thighs together, firmly gripping Uke's

FIG 206

FIG 207

upper arm between them and pulling Uke's arm downwards across his right thigh. Tori must be sufficiently close to Uke to be able to pull Uke's elbow on to the thigh or a little past it. To apply the lock, Tori maintains his pull on Uke's arm—pulling it outwards and downwards—and lifts his hips from the mat.

Applying the Lock against Resistance

The usual defence is to pull the right shoulder and arm away by turning on the right side to face Tori, so that Tori is unable to apply leverage on Uke's elbow. Tori can render this escape ineffective, however, by maintaining a constant upward pull on Uke's arm.

Uke might manage to bend his arm at the elbow and clasp his hands together against the lock: and this could succeed if Uke's arm is not firmly gripped between Tori's thighs. Tori's response to such an attempt is to slide his left forearm under Uke's forearm, clasping his own hands and pulling Uke's hands apart to apply the lock (Fig. 208). Tori should turn his arm so that the sharp side of his forearm—the thumb side—presses against the soft inside of Uke's forearm. If Uke is very strong, Tori should bring his forearm under Uke's forearm, as in Figure 208, and then place his right leg over Uke's forearm. He locks by pressing down with his leg and pulling back with his arms and body (Fig. 209). As Figures 208 and 209 show, Tori will have to sit up when attempting to separate Uke's hands. This enables him to bring the full power of his body into action by thrusting forward with his hips.

FIG 208

FIG 209

150

Variations

The angle at which Tori places
his body in relation to Uke's will
dictate the manner in which the
lock is applied. If Tori's body is
inclined towards Uke's feet, for
instance, the lock would probably
be applied over Tori's left thigh
instead of his right thigh.

FIG 210

Tori may find himself on his
back, with Uke getting set to
attack from his right side. In this
event, Tori should attempt to
bring his right leg up and place his right shin—with the leg bent
at the knee—against Uke's left hip or thigh. This is to prevent Uke
from working round to Tori's right side. At the same time, Tori
grips the end of Uke's right sleeve with his left hand and thrusts
Uke's left hip or thigh away with his right leg while pulling Uke's
right arm outwards towards his own head (Fig. 210). He now turns
on his right hip so that he is face downwards. If he continues to pull
Uke's arm outwards, gripping the upper arm tightly between his
thighs, he applies the same lock but with Uke underneath and both
contestants face downwards (Fig. 211).

The lock can be applied from either side of Uke's body. So that
if Uke pushes upwards at Tori's face or one of his shoulders when
Tori is astride him, Tori grips Uke's sleeve to pull the arm upwards
and falls on his back to the side which is being attacked, the rest of
the movements being adapted accordingly.

FIG 211

UDE-GARAMI—BENT OR FIGURE FOUR ARM LOCK

Uke is lying on his back, with Tori at his right side. To defend himself, Uke pushes at Tori's chest or shoulder with his left hand. At once, Tori grips Uke's wrist with his left hand; and, pushing outwards and down against the arm, he thrusts it flat down on the mat so that the arm is bent at right-angles at the elbow, with the forearm upwards. To assist this movement, Tori can grip the left sleeve of Uke's jacket at the elbow with his right hand. Tori's arms will be supported by the full power of his body as he thrusts forward with his hips and drives his chest down towards Uke's chest (Fig. 212).

As Uke's arm is pressed flat to the mat, Tori brings his right arm under Uke's upper arm, close to the shoulder, and grips his own left wrist. To apply the lock, Tori lifts his right wrist and forearm while holding Uke's arm flat on the mat with his left hand. He must be careful not to lift Uke's elbow, which should be kept on the mat.

The lock can be applied by Tori turning his left wrist clockwise—to pin Uke's arm to the mat—and his right wrist anti-clockwise—so that the sharp cutting edge of his right wrist at the thumb side comes into contact with Uke's arm (Fig. 213).

FIG 212

FIG 213

Applying the Lock against Resistance

If he can manage to turn his arm inwards, as if pushing at Tori, and also brace his elbow against the mat, Uke can develop a strong defence. To overcome it, Tori thrusts Uke's arm sideways, driving against it from the inside, and pushes in the same direction against

Uke's elbow with his right hand. At the same time, he digs in with his toes and thrusts his hips and body forward to bring the full power of his body into action against Uke's arm. Tori's back should be hollowed rather than curved to gain greatest effect.

Tori must follow any movement of Uke's arms, always driving against them sideways. He might even drive Uke's arms sideways with his head, still maintaining the drive from his hips.

Variations

Uke may attempt to push his arm downwards, to defend by gripping his own belt, his own right hand, or his own jacket. In such a case, Tori should push Uke's arm to the mat so that it is bent at the elbow at right-angles but with the forearm pointing towards Uke's feet. Tori then pins Uke's wrist down with his right hand, bringing his left hand under Uke's upper arm to grip his own right wrist and apply the lock.

Change of Lock

Uke may attempt to pull the arm being attacked away to his left. Tori follows this direction and thrusts the arm on to the mat so that it is stretched out straight from the shoulder to Uke's left. He then grips Uke's wrist and brings his right hand under Uke's elbow to grip his own left wrist, applying the lock by keeping Uke's arm stretched out on the mat with his left hand while lifting with his right hand. The upward pressure is applied under Uke's elbow.

If, in his defence, Uke pushes hard at Tori's chest or shoulder with his left hand, Tori should move his body back by hollowing his back—thus allowing Uke to straighten his arm. As soon as this occurs, Tori can attempt *Ude-gatame*, the description of which follows.

UDE-GATAME—STRAIGHT ARM LOCK WITH THE ARMS

Tori may be either kneeling at Uke's right side or astride Uke. In his defence, Uke pushes at Tori's chest or right shoulder with his left hand. Tori resists the pressure in order to encourage Uke to maintain the push. If he is astride Uke, he glides his right leg across Uke's body to kneel at Uke's right side. At the same time, he clasps his hands round Uke's left arm so that the cutting edge of his forearm or wrist is against Uke's arm at the elbow. Immediately, so that it synchronises with a thrust forward of his hips, Tori presses Uke's arm upwards and inwards. It is the combined hand and body movement that applies the lock. Uke's arm must be stretched upwards (Fig. 214).

FIG 214

Take note that the stretching action upon Uke's arm is very important. In some holds the grip on Uke's wrist makes this comparatively simple: but in *Ude-gatame* it can only be effected by the combined hip, trunk and arm movement, aided by a clockwise turn of the wrists. Remember that as the hips thrust forward and the back is hollowed Tori's shoulder and chest are withdrawn from Uke's pushing arm, ensuring that Uke's arm straightens.

Applying the Lock against Resistance

This is not easy. If Uke succeeds in pulling back his arm and bending the elbow, Tori can do no more than attempt to change the lock.

Variations

This is a difficult lock to apply and there are no important variations, although Tori could roll on to his back, taking Uke over with him—which might increase the pressure on Uke's arm.

Change of Lock

Uke might attempt to pull his arm away. Tori therefore takes his right leg across Uke and at once extends his right leg so that it is fully outstretched to his right front and pulls Uke's arm side-ways and outwards so that it is stretched out across his leg, preferably just above the knee (Fig. 215). Uke's elbow must be outside Tori's leg.

Tori applies the lock by pulling Uke's arm outwards and downwards across his leg. He must keep his trunk upright.

If Uke succeeds in sliding his hand down Tori's chest and bending his elbow, Tori maintains his inward pressure and stretching movement against Uke's arm, bringing his left foot round the top of Uke's head to replace it on the mat so that the back of his left thigh is across Uke's neck. He then rolls back on to the mat, maintaining the pressure and pull on Uke's arm and bringing his left knee on to the arm to add to the pressure. Figure 216 shows the position just before Tori moves his left knee into Uke's elbow.

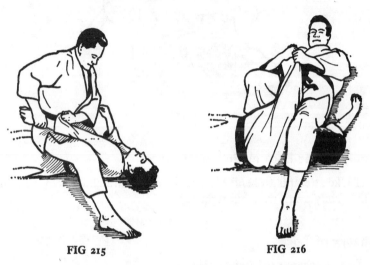

FIG 215   FIG 216

HIZA-GATAME—KNEE ARM LOCK

This lock is applied from beneath the opponent—perhaps as Uke attempts to strangle from a kneeling position between Tori's legs. It can also be applied when Tori is on his back, with Uke at, say, his right side: in which case, Tori catches the end of Uke's right sleeve with his left hand—his right holding where convenient—and draws him down while bringing his right knee under Uke's body (Fig. 217). He continues drawing Uke down, pulling Uke's right arm towards his own left shoulder and pushing Uke's legs and body away with his right knee. Uke should now be drawn to a face-down kneeling position on the mat with his arm fully outstretched, at which point

Tori brings his left knee over Uke's right elbow, or a little above it, and applies the lock by stretching Uke's arm outwards and upwards and pressing down with his knee (Fig. 218). It is not strictly necessary for Tori to grip Uke's wrist: the pull on Uke's sleeve is sufficient. However, most judomen do take a hold on the wrist.

FIG 217

Applying the Lock against Resistance

If Uke attempts to bend his arm, Tori can straighten it by pressing Uke's body away with his right leg.

Change of Lock

Tori can change to *Ashi-gatame* by straightening his left leg and sliding his left shin under Uke's neck.

If he fails to stretch out Uke's arm sufficiently, or is unable to control Uke's body, it might be possible for him to roll to his right side while maintaining the stretching action on Uke's arm. He would then turn until he is face down on Uke, pulling the attacked arm up between his legs so that he is applying *Ude-hishigi-ju-ji-*

FIG 218

156

FIG 219

gatame in a reverse position, as shown in Figure 219. Uke's arm may be locked over either thigh.

Should Uke still resist successfully, Tori might be able to pass his legs under Uke's body so that they can be used as levers. He would then roll himself and Uke over so that he is on his back with Uke, also on his back, on top of him. Uke would find it difficult to prevent this movement. Tori would then be holding Uke in *Ude-hishigi-ju-ji-gatame* (Fig. 220).

FIG 220

ASHI-GATAME—LEG ARM LOCK

This is very like *Hiza-gatame*, except that on this occasion Tori brings his left leg over Uke's outstretched right arm and passes it under Uke's face or neck (Fig. 221). The lock is applied by Tori pulling Uke's arm outwards and upwards against his own left thigh,

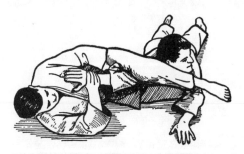

FIG 221

at the same time driving the thigh downwards by straightening his leg. The double attack against Uke's arm makes this a very powerful lock.

The information given under the sub-headings for *Hiza-gatame* applies equally to this lock.

CHAPTER XII

Shime-Waza – Neck Locking Techniques

Neck locks are divided into two classes. One is strangle locks, which check the flow of blood to the brain, and the other is choke locks, which block the breathing.

Shime-waza should be applied quickly and without warning, for if the opponent is able to anticipate the attack he may well find an opportunity to prevent it and counter with *Kansetsu-waza*. On the other hand, opportunities do arise for the attacker to apply *Kansetsu-waza* if the opponent defends himself against *Shime-waza*.

Contest Rules

Shime-waza may be applied standing.

If Uke goes down to the ground in an effort to escape, Tori may follow him down or go down with him to continue his lock.

It is forbidden to attempt to apply *Shime-waza* while lying on the back against an opponent who would then be in a position to pick up the person applying the lock. In particular, the legs must not be crossed round the opponent's body to hold him while the lock is applied. If the lock is attempted from such a position, it must be released as soon as the opponent commences to lift (Fig. 222).

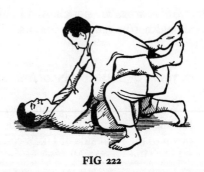

FIG 222

159

Relaxation

Relaxation is absolutely essential when applying *Shime-waza*. Figure 223 shows how, when it is stiff, Tori's wrist makes only spot contact with Uke's neck. Whereas with the wrist and arm relaxed, as in Figure 224, close and effective contact is made.

It is not easy to obtain the necessary hold for an effective strangle or choke lock. If Tori's arms and wrists are rigid, his attempt will fail. More than that, he will find that his forearms and wrists become tired, thereby greatly lessening his potential.

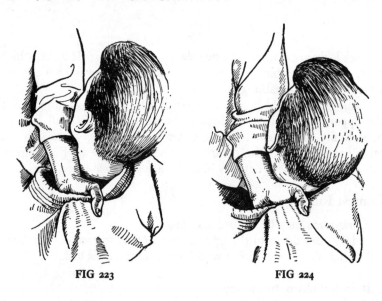

FIG 223   FIG 224

Junior Contests

Shime-waza are not allowed in junior contests, and these techniques should not be taught to juniors.

NAMI-JU-JI-JIME—NORMAL CROSS STRANGLE LOCK

With Uke on his back and Tori astride him, Tori slides his hand—for the purpose of this description let us say his right hand—deep down to the right side of Uke's collar, with the palm of the hand downwards (Fig. 225). He brings his left hand across Uke's body to

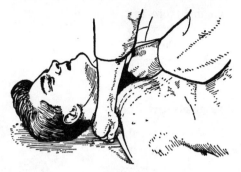

FIG 225

take a similar hold deep on the left side of Uke's collar. Tori must avoid turning his wrists so that the back of his wrist or forearm is against Uke's neck. He should have the sharp, bony edge of wrist and forearm against Uke's neck for greatest effect. The object now is to get at the carotid arteries, which run down each side of the neck slightly behind the ears. These arteries are protected by a bank of muscles which vary in strength with the individual. To displace the protection, Tori turns his wrists inwards so that the edges of his wrists—on the little-finger side—come into firm contact with Uke's neck.

This firm inward pressure must be maintained throughout. Tori then draws his wrists towards his own chest, thus drawing forward Uke's protecting muscles. Keeping up this movement compresses the arteries in Uke's neck and causes unconsciousness.

To ensure maximum leverage, Tori continues to draw his wrists forward and lowers his body forward so that the top of his head is almost on the mat above Uke's head. At the same time, he must be careful to keep his elbows close to his sides. Failure to do so will result in the lock being relaxed. Figure 226 shows the efficiency of the lock with Tori's elbows cor-

FIG 226

rectly held in. But in Figure 227
Tori has allowed his elbows to
move outwards, relaxing the pressure and allowing Uke's muscles
to move back to protect the artery.

Opportunities to apply the Lock

Although it is usually applied
when Tori is astride Uke, it
can equally well be applied
from underneath: that is, when
an opponent in an astride position
brings his head close to Tori's
head or chest.

The lock can, in fact, be applied
at almost any time when Uke's
neck is fairly close to Tori's chest
and Tori has his arms free.

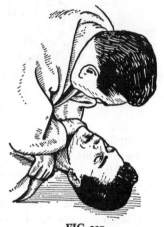

FIG 227

Applying the Lock against Resistance

From the astride position Tori can usually obtain a satisfactory
hold on Uke's collar with one hand—say his left—because this
presents no immediate danger to Uke. But his effort to bring his
right hand into action is likely to be blocked. Instead of trying for
Uke's collar in the prescribed way with his right hand, therefore,
Tori could bring his right hand and forearm under Uke's head or
neck from Uke's left side—a move which does not appear to offer much
danger to Uke. The hand should be brought through until Tori is
able to grip the back of Uke's collar as far round to Uke's right side
as he can (Fig. 228). From here Tori can, with a swift movement,
whip his arm from beneath Uke's head and into position across his
neck to apply the lock.

It is likely that Uke will tuck his chin down on to his chest to
avoid the lock. This is overcome from the astride position by applying
firm inward pressure and drawing the wrists and forearms forward in
the usual way—but this time against the sides of Uke's jaw. Maintaining the inward pressure, Tori turns his wrists and forearms so that
Uke's chin is pushed or rolled upwards and he is able to apply his lock.
Tori's wrist movement here is to turn one wrist in a clockwise direction

and the other anticlockwise.

Uke might slide his wrist or forearm between his neck and Tori's attacking arm, perhaps tucking in his chin as well. If Tori has the correct hold on Uke's collar, he applies the inward pressure and rolls on his side. Assuming that he rolls to his right side, he brings his right foot up and presses it against Uke's left thigh (Fig. 229). To apply the lock, Tori straightens his right leg and thus thrusts Uke's body out straight. This also has the effect of throwing Uke's head back, allowing the application of the lock.

FIG 228

FIG 229

Opportunities to apply Arm Locks

When applying *Nami-ju-ji-jime* Tori must keep his arms well bent at the elbows. The lock cannot be applied with straight arms and Uke may therefore move away from Tori in an effort to straighten Tori's arms. If Uke pushes Tori away, Tori should be alert for an opportunity to attempt a form of *Ude-hishigi-ju-ji-gatame*—which would necessitate him moving to Uke's side from his astride position.

Uke, perhaps being extra careful, might push away with the elbow of his pushing arm kept close to his side. Nevertheless, this could give an opening for *Ude-garame*—in which case, Tori would have to move one leg across Uke's body so that both his legs and hips were on the mat on the opposite side of Uke to the arm being attacked.

Danger to Tori of Arm Locks

The danger arises when Tori attacks from too far out, tending to straighten his arms. From Uke's side he may open himself to *Hiza-gatame* or *Ashi-gatame*. This form of lock could also be applied when Tori is astride if Uke is able to bring one knee under Tori's leg and thrust him downwards.

GYAKU-JU-JI-JIME—REVERSE CROSS NECK LOCK

But for the form of grip on Uke's collar, this lock and *Nami-ju-ji-jime* are identical. The difference is that Tori grips Uke's collar with his fingers inside the collar and his thumbs outside. The lock is applied with the thumb-side cutting edges of the wrists and forearms.

Which of the two locks to apply is a matter for personal choice. I find *Nami-ju-ji-jime* easier . . . but a great many prefer *Gyaku-ju-ji-jime*.

Information under sub-headings for *Nami-ju-ji-jime* applies equally here.

KATA-JU-JI-JIME—HALF CROSS NECK LOCK

A combination of *Nami-ju-ji-jime* and *Gyaku-ju-ji-jime*, this lock helps to overcome the problem of getting the second hand into position after the positioning of the first hand has betrayed the intention. One hand adopts the *Nami* (thumbs inside) hold while the other takes the *Gyaku* (fingers inside) hold. Usually, the hand nearest Uke's chin takes the *Nami* hold.

It is simpler to take the *Gyaku* hold first, leaving the *Nami* hold to be taken when the opportunity occurs during the struggle.

Again, the *Nami-ju-ji-jime* sub-headings will apply.

OKURI-ERI-JIME—SLIDING COLLAR OR LAPEL NECK LOCK

This lock can be used if Uke adopts what he considers a safe defensive position—posssibly with his arms crossed over his throat, holding his own collar.

For the purpose of practice, Uke kneels on the mat with Tori behind him. Tori slides his left hand under Uke's left armpit, reaches across his chest and grips Uke's right lapel fairly high up. At the same time, he throws his right arm round Uke's neck and takes hold of the left side of Uke's collar as far round as possible (Fig. 230). The right hand hold is with the thumb inside the collar, so that the thumb edge of Tori's wrist and forearm is against Uke's throat. To apply the lock, Tori pulls evenly with both hands in a circular movement

FIG 230

to Uke's rear, so that his right wrist and arm wind round Uke's neck and his left hand pulls Uke's jacket to his left to prevent it riding round with the pull of the right hand.

Opportunities to apply the Lock

Tori will never find Uke conveniently kneeling upright in a contest. An opening will, therefore, have to be sought. It could present itself during a struggle on the ground when Uke half turns away from Tori. Perhaps Tori is attempting *Yoko-shiho-gatame* from Uke's right side and Uke turns on his left side to avoid being held. Tori can at once slide his left arm under Uke's neck and left armpit to grip the right

FIG 231

side of Uke's lapel (Fig. 231). He will then easily be able to bring his right arm over his opponent's throat and grip his left lapel (Fig. 232). To apply the lock, Tori rolls on his back, taking Uke with him so that Uke is face upwards on top of him. Tori then traps Uke's legs with his own in order to obtain full control (Fig. 233).

FIG 232

FIG 233

Applying the Lock against Resistance

If Uke adopts a kneeling defensive position, an opportunity to apply the lock still exists. Tori moves to Uke's left side and slides his left arm under Uke's left armpit to grip Uke's right lapel. Then he slides his right hand over Uke's right shoulder and round his neck to grip Uke's left lapel (Fig. 234). He applies the lock by throwing himself back and taking Uke with him into the position shown in Figure 233.

Uke may instinctively tuck in his chin and cover his neck with

FIG 234

his hands. This does not matter. The fall back is usually enough to flick Uke's head back; but additionally, Tori can turn his right arm in a clockwise direction to force Uke's chin up.

Opportunities for Arm Locks

Assuming Tori has brought his left arm under Uke's left armpit, Uke will have to use his left hand with his right to grip Tori's right sleeve in an attempt to relax the pressure. As he does this, Tori can slide his left arm up Uke's left arm to straighten it and lock it (Fig. 235). The illustration shows a kneeling position to make the movement clear. Tori will have to pin Uke's body and may do this by rolling himself and Uke over so that they are face down on the mat, with Uke underneath. Tori then draws Uke's arm upwards into the lock, changing his right hand position as the opportunity occurs (Fig. 236).

FIG 235

FIG 236

Danger to Tori of Arm Locks or Holds

Being behind Uke, Tori is in no danger of being arm-locked; but Uke might be able to turn and apply a hold down. It could happen like this: Tori attempts *Okuri-eri-jime*, but Uke manages to resist by tucking down his chin and holding off the pressure of Tori's right arm with his own arms. As Tori falls or is pushed back, Uke whips over on to his right side, gripping Tori's right arm with his left hand and applying *Kesa-gatame*. Uke remains open to a neck lock and his right arm will be in a weak position, but he will naturally attempt to adjust this during the struggle.

KATA-HA-JIME—SINGLE WING NECK LOCK

To practice this lock, Tori stations himself behind Uke and brings his right arm over Uke's right shoulder and round his neck to grip the left side of Uke's collar as far round as possible. He brings his left arm under Uke's left armpit from behind and slides it behind Uke's neck, with the cutting edge of wrist and forearm on the little-finger side against the back of Uke's neck (Fig. 237). To apply the lock, Tori pulls round Uke's neck with his right hand—turned so that the cutting edge of wrist and forearm on the

FIG 237

thumb side is in contact with Uke's neck—and pushes forward with his left hand. His arms move towards each other like the blades of a pair of scissors. To get the full power of his hips and body behind the movement of his left arm, Tori thrusts his hips forward and takes his left shoulder back.

Opportunities to apply the Lock

As for *Okuri-eri-jime*.

Opportunities for Arm Locks

As for *Okuri-eri-jime*, with the added advantage that Uke's left arm is already straightened and therefore more vulnerable.

Danger to Tori of Arm Locks or Holds

There is no danger of arm locks; and, since the pinning of Uke's left arm prohibits any movement to his right, little danger from *Kesa-gatame* exists.

HADAKA-JIME—NAKED NECK LOCK

This lock is applied from behind Uke, and for the purpose of practice Uke seats himself on the mat. Tori throws his right arm round Uke's neck with the cutting edge of wrist and forearm on the thumb side against his throat. He then clasps his right hand with his left hand just above Uke's left collar bone. To apply the lock, Tori brings his head over Uke's left shoulder so that his own right shoulder presses against the back of Uke's head, at the same time drawing his right arm back (Fig. 238). The combined backward pressure of Tori's right forearm and forward pressure of his shoulder forces submission.

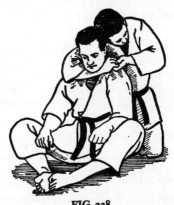

FIG 238

Variations

Tori brings his right arm round Uke's neck as described above but brings his left elbow up above Uke's collar bone and places his right hand against the upper part of his own left forearm just below the elbow. He places his left hand behind Uke's neck (Fig. 239). The lock is applied by backward pressure of the right forearm and forward pressure of the left hand against the back of Uke's neck.

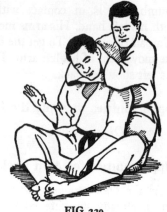

FIG 239

Opportunities to apply the Lock

Since Tori must attack from behind, he will not find it easy to attain the best position; but opportunities present themselves if Uke adopts a defensive position on hands and knees or attempts to escape from a hold down.

Applying the Lock against Resistance

Uke's natural reaction is to tuck his chin down on his chest. This is overcome by Tori turning his right arm to roll Uke's chin backwards and then slipping his arm underneath it. Or Tori could thrust his hips forward and roll on to his back, throwing Uke's head back. But if he does this, Tori will have to use his legs to pin Uke's legs and prevent him from rolling away.

Opportunities for Arm Locks

These are few. It is possible that Uke, having successfully blocked the neck lock for a moment by tucking his chin down on his chest, might bring his left hand and arm up to pull Tori's right jacket sleeve forward to relax the pressure on his neck or chin. Tori can then release the neck lock with his left hand and bring that hand under Uke's left armpit to straighten Uke's arm and pull it backwards. During this, Tori's right hand can be left round Uke's neck—perhaps gripping Uke's jacket above the left shoulder to maintain control. Tori now leans back, by thrusting his hip forward, and brings his right arm over

Uke's head to join his left, so that both hands are gripping Uke's left arm, and turns himself face down on the mat with Uke face down beneath him. A form of face down *Ude-hishigi-ju-ji-gatame* is applied (Fig. 240). However, Tori may prefer to hold Uke over with his left arm only and use his right arm as a support. This must exert control also (Fig. 241).

FIG 240

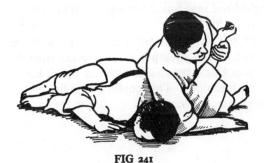

FIG 241

Danger to Tori of Arm Locks or Holds

The danger of counter locks is very slight. Uke's immediate action must be to free himself from the attempted neck lock. By tucking his chin down on his chest and pulling Tori's right sleeve forward to relax the pressure, he might be able to turn sharply to his right—using as much hip movement as his position allows—to throw Tori back on to the mat to his right side. He can then adopt *Kesa-gatame* at Tori's right. Tori's neck lock will not have been fully broken and might still be applied despite this hold down.

Use of the Hands in Shime-Waza

I am often asked which hand should be brought into action first when attempting a neck lock. In theory, it does not matter. But in practice it can make quite a difference.

The first essential is to maintain control of Uke. Therefore, if Uke's body is controlled or pinned only on one side, the hand which must come into action first is that which will control or pin the other side. Let us take an example. In *Nami-ju-ji-jime* Tori is at Uke's right, controlling that side by pressing his right knee down on Uke's body. If Tori

FIG 242

brings his right hand into action to grip the right side of Uke's collar, Uke can escape to his left. But if Tori first uses his left hand to hold the left side of Uke's collar, Uke will be pinned on both sides (Fig. 242).

It is often best, when attempting *Shime-waza* from either front or rear, to first grip Uke's jacket at a position which has nothing at all to do with the technique. This could be useful bluff; but its real purpose is to gain initial control.

CHAPTER XIII

Contest Work on the Ground

Hands and Knees Defence

Uke crouches on his knees with his head kept low and possibly with his arms across his throat to prevent a strangle lock (Fig. 243).

Although frequently seen in contests, this is not a strong defensive position and any experienced judoman should be able to break it up. To this end, Tori will find arm locks effective.

With Uke in the position shown in Figure 243, it will be Tori's object to persuade him to place the hand nearest Tori on the mat. This can be done by attempting to roll Uke over on to his back. If, therefore, Tori is at Uke's left side, he should attempt to roll Uke to his left and on to his back, bringing Uke's left hand on to the

FIG 243

FIG 244

173

mat in defence. So Tori brings his left arm under Uke's left armpit and places his hand or forearm on the back of Uke's neck so that he can powerfully lever Uke's arm upwards and outwards (Fig. 244). At the same time, he slides his right foot under Uke's body and pushes Uke's right arm outwards with his foot, causing Uke to collapse face down on the mat with his left arm outstretched to his left. To apply his lock, Tori brings his left foot across the back of Uke's arm, bending it over the arm and pushing the arm upwards with both hands (Fig. 245).

FIG 245

Another lock of a similar nature can be applied from the same position. Tori grips Uke's left sleeve and persuades him to bring his left hand outwards and down on to the mat. He then brings his right leg over Uke's left arm, close to the shoulder (Fig. 246), and turns so that he almost has his back to Uke's body (Fig. 247). Tori then rolls himself backwards, taking Uke with him. His grip on Uke's jacket and his leg over Uke's arm will force Uke down on to his back with his left arm pulled out straight (Fig. 248). *Ju–ii-gatame* is very like this lock.

FIG 246

FIG 247   FIG 248

Moving an Opponent who is Astride

If the attacker—in this case, Uke—has taken up the correct position, high up on his opponent's body and with his knees pressing firmly into his opponent's armpits, he will not be easy to move. And Tori, in trying to dislodge him, must be careful not to offer opportunities for arm locks.

Tori's first move should be to get Uke further down his body—because the nearer he is to Tori's hips the more effect will Tori's struggles have upon him. Therefore, Tori bridges his body, assisting the upward movement perhaps by pushing on Uke's hips or the sides of his body. Having succeeded in shifting Uke's position, Tori continues his bridge, at the same time gripping the end of one of Uke's sleeves—the right, say. At the top of the bridge, Tori turns his body to his left by thrusting his left hip back until it is below his right hip —bringing the full power of his hips into play—and at the same time thrusts Uke's right arm hard across his body. This should roll Uke off.

When Uke is near Tori's hips it might be possible for Tori to half turn on his side—his right side, for example—and bring his right leg up so that his right knee is above Uke's left thigh. By thrusting down with his right leg against Uke's left thigh, Tori should be able to push Uke away. Escaping in this way, Tori then has a good chance of applying an arm lock.

Passing an Opponent's Legs in Groundwork

The legs are an important weapon in groundwork, and the defender attempts to pivot so as to place his legs between himself and his attacker. The defender should therefore keep his legs well drawn back so that his opponent cannot catch a foot or lower leg with a hand and so get past him.

Uke, on the ground, will attempt to push Tori away with one foot. But if Tori moves close in with, say, his right foot, he can allow Uke to push against it without any risk (Fig. 249). Tori then brings his left foot up close to Uke's side (Fig. 250) and thrusts his right foot well back, to drop immediately into a hold down position (Fig. 251). Tori can use his arms to push Uke's legs aside, keeping his arms fairly straight and employing a sweeping motion.

FIG 249

FIG 250

FIG 251

Use of the Hips in Groundwork

The principles of groundwork and those of *Tachi-waza* are identical and are particularly noteworthy regarding movement of the hips. Free movement and control of the hips is essential when attacking, and drive from the hips is of vital importance in defence. Briefly, the following points should be remembered when attacking:

Osaekomi-waza—Holding Down

The hips must be relaxed and must rest on the mat. Any body movements made when holding should be made from the hips.

Kansetsu-waza—Locks on Joints

A great number of locks are applied by Tori using his arms to stretch out Uke's arm and then completing the lock with his hips. Typical examples are *Ju-ji-gatame* and *Ude-gatame*. Thrust from the hips must be added to the strength of the arms.

Shime-waza—Neck Locks

The thrust of the hips—or at least their position—can make the difference between failure and success.

Use of the Opponent's Belt

Use of the opponent's belt is important, and it is of particular value on the ground. In *Tachi-waza* it is strictly limited by the rules.

The rules state that it is forbidden to hold the belt "continuously". It may be held in the application of throws such as *Uki-goshi* and *O-goshi*—but only during the actual attempt. A common interpretation of this ruling is that such a hold can be maintained for about three seconds.

Breaking Holds

A judo hold can be likened to a beam-and-fulcrum relationship in which Tori is the beam and Uke the fulcrum, the hold being effective as long as the beam is off centre to one side or the other of the fulcrum. To break the hold, the fulcrum must regain the centre of the beam. Therefore, Uke must either move the fulcrum—himself—or persuade the beam—Tori—to move willingly. Let us say then, that Uke is held with *Kesa-gatame*, Tori being at his right. The position is that of a beam which has tipped to one side of the fulcrum and will not pivot (Fig. 252). Uke's first move is to bring his left arm round Tori and grasp Tori's belt in order to gain as much control as possible over Tori's hips. His right hand also holds Tori's belt or jacket. He might try pushing Tori to his, Uke's, right; and should Tori

FIG 252

push back—that is, push the beam to Uke's left—the seesaw may become sufficiently well balanced for Uke to roll Tori over his body and so escape (Fig. 253).

If this does not work, Uke must move himself. So he bridges his body, lifting both himself and Tori. Relaxing, he will make a momentary gap between himself and Tori—and he should use this to slip his body under Tori's by moving his hips to his right. The gap can be increased by Uke thrusting upwards as he bridges his body. As soon as Uke has moved his hips under Tori's body, he holds Tori tightly to him and, by pivoting his hips to his left, may well succeed in rolling Tori over him. A second effort may be necessary before Uke feels that he is sufficiently under Tori to make the seesaw, or roll, effective.

The same method is applied to *Kami-shiho-gatame*, in which Tori can defend effectively against pushes to left or right (Fig. 254), but

FIG 253

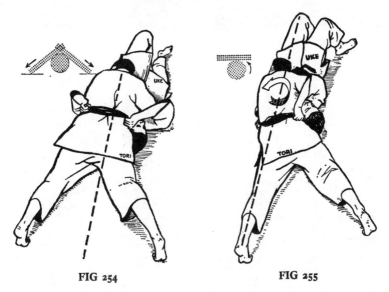

FIG 254   FIG 255

this time Uke manoeuvres so that if a line were drawn down the centre of his body it would continue along one of Tori's legs. At this stage, the "beam" might be well enough balanced for the hold to be broken (Fig. 255). Uke's object is to get into such a position that the leg which Tori is using as a lever suddenly becomes ineffectual (Fig. 256).

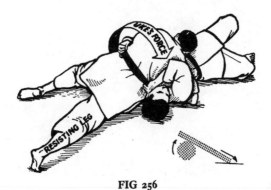

FIG 256

REFEREE'S CALLS

In all judo contests the referee gives his instructions in Japanese. The calls are as follows.

HAJIME	Commence.
MATE	Break.
WAZA-ARI	Near Point.
IPPON	Point.
WAZA-ARI AWASETE IPPON	Point scored from two *Waza-ari*.
OSAEKOMI	Holding.
TOKETA	Hold Broken.
FUSENSHO	A win by default—the opponent having failed to arrive.
HANTEI	Request for the judges to show their decision.
SONO-MAMA	Keep still—used, for example, when a hold down is applied close to the edge of the mat and the referee wishes to bring the contestants into the centre.
YOSHI	Carry on—usually used after a hold down has been "frozen" by the referee.
YUSHI-GACHI	Win by superiority.
SORE-MADE	Stop—end of contest.

The time-keeper's call is of no significance to the contestants. They continue the contest until the referee orders "Sore-made".

A CATALOGUE OF SELECTED DOVER BOOKS
IN ALL FIELDS OF INTEREST

A CATALOGUE OF SELECTED DOVER BOOKS
IN ALL FIELDS OF INTEREST

AMERICA'S OLD MASTERS, James T. Flexner. Four men emerged unexpectedly from provincial 18th century America to leadership in European art: Benjamin West, J. S. Copley, C. R. Peale, Gilbert Stuart. Brilliant coverage of lives and contributions. Revised, 1967 edition. 69 plates. 365pp. of text.
21806-6 Paperbound $3.00

FIRST FLOWERS OF OUR WILDERNESS: AMERICAN PAINTING, THE COLONIAL PERIOD, James T. Flexner. Painters, and regional painting traditions from earliest Colonial times up to the emergence of Copley, West and Peale Sr., Foster, Gustavus Hesselius, Feke, John Smibert and many anonymous painters in the primitive manner. Engaging presentation, with 162 illustrations. xxii + 368pp.
22180-6 Paperbound $3.50

THE LIGHT OF DISTANT SKIES: AMERICAN PAINTING, 1760-1835, James T. Flexner. The great generation of early American painters goes to Europe to learn and to teach: West, Copley, Gilbert Stuart and others. Allston, Trumbull, Morse; also contemporary American painters—primitives, derivatives, academics—who remained in America. 102 illustrations. xiii + 306pp.
22179-2 Paperbound $3.00

A HISTORY OF THE RISE AND PROGRESS OF THE ARTS OF DESIGN IN THE UNITED STATES, William Dunlap. Much the richest mine of information on early American painters, sculptors, architects, engravers, miniaturists, etc. The only source of information for scores of artists, the major primary source for many others. Unabridged reprint of rare original 1834 edition, with new introduction by James T. Flexner, and 394 new illustrations. Edited by Rita Weiss. 6⅝ x 9⅝.
21695-0, 21696-9, 21697-7 Three volumes, Paperbound $13.50

EPOCHS OF CHINESE AND JAPANESE ART, Ernest F. Fenollosa. From primitive Chinese art to the 20th century, thorough history, explanation of every important art period and form, including Japanese woodcuts; main stress on China and Japan, but Tibet, Korea also included. Still unexcelled for its detailed, rich coverage of cultural background, aesthetic elements, diffusion studies, particularly of the historical period. 2nd, 1913 edition. 242 illustrations. lii + 439pp. of text.
20364-6, 20365-4 Two volumes, Paperbound $6.00

THE GENTLE ART OF MAKING ENEMIES, James A. M. Whistler. Greatest wit of his day deflates Oscar Wilde, Ruskin, Swinburne; strikes back at inane critics, exhibitions, art journalism; aesthetics of impressionist revolution in most striking form. Highly readable classic by great painter. Reproduction of edition designed by Whistler. Introduction by Alfred Werner. xxxvi + 334pp.
21875-9 Paperbound $2.50

ALPHABETS AND ORNAMENTS, Ernst Lehner. Well-known pictorial source for decorative alphabets, script examples, cartouches, frames, decorative title pages, calligraphic initials, borders, similar material. 14th to 19th century, mostly European. Useful in almost any graphic arts designing, varied styles. 750 illustrations. 256pp. 7 x 10. 21905-4 Paperbound $4.00

PAINTING: A CREATIVE APPROACH, Norman Colquhoun. For the beginner simple guide provides an instructive approach to painting: major stumbling blocks for beginner; overcoming them, technical points; paints and pigments; oil painting; watercolor and other media and color. New section on "plastic" paints. Glossary. Formerly *Paint Your Own Pictures.* 221pp. 22000-1 Paperbound $1.75

THE ENJOYMENT AND USE OF COLOR, Walter Sargent. Explanation of the relations between colors themselves and between colors in nature and art, including hundreds of little-known facts about color values, intensities, effects of high and low illumination, complementary colors. Many practical hints for painters, references to great masters. 7 color plates, 29 illustrations. x + 274pp.
20944-X Paperbound $2.75

THE NOTEBOOKS OF LEONARDO DA VINCI, compiled and edited by Jean Paul Richter. 1566 extracts from original manuscripts reveal the full range of Leonardo's versatile genius: all his writings on painting, sculpture, architecture, anatomy, astronomy, geography, topography, physiology, mining, music, etc., in both Italian and English, with 186 plates of manuscript pages and more than 500 additional drawings. Includes studies for the Last Supper, the lost Sforza monument, and other works. Total of xlvii + 866pp. $7\frac{7}{8}$ x $10\frac{3}{4}$.
22572-0, 22573-9 Two volumes, Paperbound $10.00

MONTGOMERY WARD CATALOGUE OF 1895. Tea gowns, yards of flannel and pillow-case lace, stereoscopes, books of gospel hymns, the New Improved Singer Sewing Machine, side saddles, milk skimmers, straight-edged razors, high-button shoes, spittoons, and on and on . . . listing some 25,000 items, practically all illustrated. Essential to the shoppers of the 1890's, it is our truest record of the spirit of the period. Unaltered reprint of Issue No. 57, Spring and Summer 1895. Introduction by Boris Emmet. Innumerable illustrations. xiii + 624pp. $8\frac{1}{2}$ x $11\frac{5}{8}$.
22377-9 Paperbound $6.95

THE CRYSTAL PALACE EXHIBITION ILLUSTRATED CATALOGUE (LONDON, 1851). One of the wonders of the modern world—the Crystal Palace Exhibition in which all the nations of the civilized world exhibited their achievements in the arts and sciences—presented in an equally important illustrated catalogue. More than 1700 items pictured with accompanying text—ceramics, textiles, cast-iron work, carpets, pianos, sleds, razors, wall-papers, billiard tables, beehives, silverware and hundreds of other artifacts—represent the focal point of Victorian culture in the Western World. Probably the largest collection of Victorian decorative art ever assembled— indispensable for antiquarians and designers. Unabridged republication of the Art-Journal Catalogue of the Great Exhibition of 1851, with all terminal essays. New introduction by John Gloag, F.S.A. xxxiv + 426pp. 9 x 12.
22503-8 Paperbound $4.50

THE RED FAIRY BOOK, Andrew Lang. Lang's color fairy books have long been children's favorites. This volume includes Rapunzel, Jack and the Bean-stalk and 35 other stories, familiar and unfamiliar. 4 plates, 93 illustrations x + 367pp.

21673-X Paperbound $2.50

THE BLUE FAIRY BOOK, Andrew Lang. Lang's tales come from all countries and all times. Here are 37 tales from Grimm, the Arabian Nights, Greek Mythology, and other fascinating sources. 8 plates, 130 illustrations. xi + 390pp.

21437-0 Paperbound $2.50

HOUSEHOLD STORIES BY THE BROTHERS GRIMM. Classic English-language edition of the well-known tales — Rumpelstiltskin, Snow White, Hansel and Gretel, The Twelve Brothers, Faithful John, Rapunzel, Tom Thumb (52 stories in all). Translated into simple, straightforward English by Lucy Crane. Ornamented with headpieces, vignettes, elaborate decorative initials and a dozen full-page illustrations by Walter Crane. x + 269pp.   21080-4 Paperbound $2.50

THE MERRY ADVENTURES OF ROBIN HOOD, Howard Pyle. The finest modern versions of the traditional ballads and tales about the great English outlaw. Howard Pyle's complete prose version, with every word, every illustration of the first edition. Do not confuse this facsimile of the original (1883) with modern editions that change text or illustrations. 23 plates plus many page decorations. xxii + 296pp.

22043-5 Paperbound $2.50

THE STORY OF KING ARTHUR AND HIS KNIGHTS, Howard Pyle. The finest children's version of the life of King Arthur; brilliantly retold by Pyle, with 48 of his most imaginative illustrations. xviii + 313pp. 6⅛ x 9¼.

21445-1 Paperbound $2.50

THE WONDERFUL WIZARD OF OZ, L. Frank Baum. America's finest children's book in facsimile of first edition with all Denslow illustrations in full color. The edition a child should have. Introduction by Martin Gardner. 23 color plates, scores of drawings. iv + 267pp.   20691-2 Paperbound $2.50

THE MARVELOUS LAND OF OZ, L. Frank Baum. The second Oz book, every bit as imaginative as the Wizard. The hero is a boy named Tip, but the Scarecrow and the Tin Woodman are back, as is the Oz magic. 16 color plates, 120 drawings by John R. Neill. 287pp.   20692-0 Paperbound $2.50

THE MAGICAL MONARCH OF MO, L. Frank Baum. Remarkable adventures in a land even stranger than Oz. The best of Baum's books not in the Oz series. 15 color plates and dozens of drawings by Frank Verbeck. xviii + 237pp.

21892-9 Paperbound $2.25

THE BAD CHILD'S BOOK OF BEASTS, MORE BEASTS FOR WORSE CHILDREN, A MORAL ALPHABET, Hilaire Belloc. Three complete humor classics in one volume. Be kind to the frog, and do not call him names . . . and 28 other whimsical animals. Familiar favorites and some not so well known. Illustrated by Basil Blackwell. 156pp.   (USO) 20749-8 Paperbound $1.50

THE ARCHITECTURE OF COUNTRY HOUSES, Andrew J. Downing. Together with Vaux's *Villas and Cottages* this is the basic book for Hudson River Gothic architecture of the middle Victorian period. Full, sound discussions of general aspects of housing, architecture, style, decoration, furnishing, together with scores of detailed house plans, illustrations of specific buildings, accompanied by full text. Perhaps the most influential single American architectural book. 1850 edition. Introduction by J. Stewart Johnson. 321 figures, 34 architectural designs. xvi + 560pp.
22003-6 Paperbound $4.00

LOST EXAMPLES OF COLONIAL ARCHITECTURE, John Mead Howells. Full-page photographs of buildings that have disappeared or been so altered as to be denatured, including many designed by major early American architects. 245 plates. xvii + 248pp. 7⅞ x 10¾.
21143-6 Paperbound $3.50

DOMESTIC ARCHITECTURE OF THE AMERICAN COLONIES AND OF THE EARLY REPUBLIC, Fiske Kimball. Foremost architect and restorer of Williamsburg and Monticello covers nearly 200 homes between 1620-1825. Architectural details, construction, style features, special fixtures, floor plans, etc. Generally considered finest work in its area. 219 illustrations of houses, doorways, windows, capital mantels. xx + 314pp. 7⅞ x 10¾.
21743-4 Paperbound $4.00

EARLY AMERICAN ROOMS: 1650-1858, edited by Russell Hawes Kettell. Tour of 12 rooms, each representative of a different era in American history and each furnished, decorated, designed and occupied in the style of the era. 72 plans and elevations, 8-page color section, etc., show fabrics, wall papers, arrangements, etc. Full descriptive text. xvii + 200pp. of text. 8⅜ x 11¼.
21633-0 Paperbound $5.00

THE FITZWILLIAM VIRGINAL BOOK, edited by J. Fuller Maitland and W. B. Squire. Full modern printing of famous early 17th-century ms. volume of 300 works by Morley, Byrd, Bull, Gibbons, etc. For piano or other modern keyboard instrument; easy to read format. xxxvi + 938pp. 8⅜ x 11.
21068-5, 21069-3 Two volumes, Paperbound $10.00

KEYBOARD MUSIC, Johann Sebastian Bach. Bach Gesellschaft edition. A rich selection of Bach's masterpieces for the harpsichord: the six English Suites, six French Suites, the six Partitas (Clavierübung part I), the Goldberg Variations (Clavierübung part IV), the fifteen Two-Part Inventions and the fifteen Three-Part Sinfonias. Clearly reproduced on large sheets with ample margins; eminently playable. vi + 312pp. 8⅛ x 11.
22360-4 Paperbound $5.00

THE MUSIC OF BACH: AN INTRODUCTION, Charles Sanford Terry. A fine, nontechnical introduction to Bach's music, both instrumental and vocal. Covers organ music, chamber music, passion music, other types. Analyzes themes, developments, innovations. x + 114pp.
21075-8 Paperbound $1.25

BEETHOVEN AND HIS NINE SYMPHONIES, Sir George Grove. Noted British musicologist provides best history, analysis, commentary on symphonies. Very thorough, rigorously accurate; necessary to both advanced student and amateur music lover. 436 musical passages. vii + 407 pp.
20334-4 Paperbound $2.75

VISUAL ILLUSIONS: THEIR CAUSES, CHARACTERISTICS, AND APPLICATIONS, Matthew Luckiesh. Thorough description and discussion of optical illusion, geometric and perspective, particularly; size and shape distortions, illusions of color, of motion; natural illusions; use of illusion in art and magic, industry, etc. Most useful today with op art, also for classical art. Scores of effects illustrated. Introduction by William H. Ittleson. 100 illustrations. xxi + 252pp.

21530-X Paperbound $2.00

A HANDBOOK OF ANATOMY FOR ART STUDENTS, Arthur Thomson. Thorough, virtually exhaustive coverage of skeletal structure, musculature, etc. Full text, supplemented by anatomical diagrams and drawings and by photographs of undraped figures. Unique in its comparison of male and female forms, pointing out differences of contour, texture, form. 211 figures, 40 drawings, 86 photographs. xx + 459pp. 5⅜ x 8⅜.

21163-0 Paperbound $3.50

150 MASTERPIECES OF DRAWING, Selected by Anthony Toney. Full page reproductions of drawings from the early 16th to the end of the 18th century, all beautifully reproduced: Rembrandt, Michelangelo, Dürer, Fragonard, Urs, Graf, Wouwerman, many others. First-rate browsing book, model book for artists. xviii + 150pp. 8⅜ x 11¼.

21032-4 Paperbound $2.50

THE LATER WORK OF AUBREY BEARDSLEY, Aubrey Beardsley. Exotic, erotic, ironic masterpieces in full maturity: Comedy Ballet, Venus and Tannhauser, Pierrot, Lysistrata, Rape of the Lock, Savoy material, Ali Baba, Volpone, etc. This material revolutionized the art world, and is still powerful, fresh, brilliant. With *The Early Work*, all Beardsley's finest work. 174 plates, 2 in color. xiv + 176pp. 8⅛ x 11.

21817-1 Paperbound $3.00

DRAWINGS OF REMBRANDT, Rembrandt van Rijn. Complete reproduction of fabulously rare edition by Lippmann and Hofstede de Groot, completely reedited, updated, improved by Prof. Seymour Slive, Fogg Museum. Portraits, Biblical sketches, landscapes, Oriental types, nudes, episodes from classical mythology—All Rembrandt's fertile genius. Also selection of drawings by his pupils and followers. "Stunning volumes," *Saturday Review*. 550 illustrations. lxxviii + 552pp. 9⅛ x 12¼.

21485-0, 21486-9 Two volumes, Paperbound $10.00

THE DISASTERS OF WAR, Francisco Goya. One of the masterpieces of Western civilization—83 etchings that record Goya's shattering, bitter reaction to the Napoleonic war that swept through Spain after the insurrection of 1808 and to war in general. Reprint of the first edition, with three additional plates from Boston's Museum of Fine Arts. All plates facsimile size. Introduction by Philip Hofer, Fogg Museum. v + 97pp. 9⅜ x 8¼.

21872-4 Paperbound $2.00

GRAPHIC WORKS OF ODILON REDON. Largest collection of Redon's graphic works ever assembled: 172 lithographs, 28 etchings and engravings, 9 drawings. These include some of his most famous works. All the plates from *Odilon Redon: oeuvre graphique complet*, plus additional plates. New introduction and caption translations by Alfred Werner. 209 illustrations. xxvii + 209pp. 9⅛ x 12¼.

21966-8 Paperbound $4.00

MATHEMATICAL PUZZLES FOR BEGINNERS AND ENTHUSIASTS, Geoffrey Mott-Smith. 189 puzzles from easy to difficult—involving arithmetic, logic, algebra, properties of digits, probability, etc.—for enjoyment and mental stimulus. Explanation of mathematical principles behind the puzzles. 135 illustrations. viii + 248pp.
20198-8 Paperbound $1.75

PAPER FOLDING FOR BEGINNERS, William D. Murray and Francis J. Rigney. Easiest book on the market, clearest instructions on making interesting, beautiful origami. Sail boats, cups, roosters, frogs that move legs, bonbon boxes, standing birds, etc. 40 projects; more than 275 diagrams and photographs. 94pp.
20713-7 Paperbound $1.00

TRICKS AND GAMES ON THE POOL TABLE, Fred Herrmann. 79 tricks and games— some solitaires, some for two or more players, some competitive games—to entertain you between formal games. Mystifying shots and throws, unusual caroms, tricks involving such props as cork, coins, a hat, etc. Formerly *Fun on the Pool Table*. 77 figures. 95pp.
21814-7 Paperbound $1.00

HAND SHADOWS TO BE THROWN UPON THE WALL: A SERIES OF NOVEL AND AMUSING FIGURES FORMED BY THE HAND, Henry Bursill. Delightful picturebook from great-grandfather's day shows how to make 18 different hand shadows: a bird that flies, duck that quacks, dog that wags his tail, camel, goose, deer, boy, turtle, etc. Only book of its sort. vi + 33pp. 6½ x 9¼. 21779-5 Paperbound $1.00

WHITTLING AND WOODCARVING, E. J. Tangerman. 18th printing of best book on market. "If you can cut a potato you can carve" toys and puzzles, chains, chessmen, caricatures, masks, frames, woodcut blocks, surface patterns, much more. Information on tools, woods, techniques. Also goes into serious wood sculpture from Middle Ages to present, East and West. 464 photos, figures. x + 293pp.
20965-2 Paperbound $2.00

HISTORY OF PHILOSOPHY, Julián Marias. Possibly the clearest, most easily followed, best planned, most useful one-volume history of philosophy on the market; neither skimpy nor overfull. Full details on system of every major philosopher and dozens of less important thinkers from pre-Socratics up to Existentialism and later. Strong on many European figures usually omitted. Has gone through dozens of editions in Europe. 1966 edition, translated by Stanley Appelbaum and Clarence Strowbridge. xviii + 505pp. 21739-6 Paperbound $3.00

YOGA: A SCIENTIFIC EVALUATION, Kovoor T. Behanan. Scientific but non-technical study of physiological results of yoga exercises; done under auspices of Yale U. Relations to Indian thought, to psychoanalysis, etc. 16 photos. xxiii + 270pp.
20505-3 Paperbound $2.50

Prices subject to change without notice.
Available at your book dealer or write for free catalogue to Dept. GI, Dover Publications, Inc., 180 Varick St., N. Y., N. Y. 10014. Dover publishes more than 150 books each year on science, elementary and advanced mathematics, biology, music, art, literary history, social sciences and other areas.